MAKING PATRIOTS

MAKING
PATRIOTS

Walter Berns

THE UNIVERSITY OF CHICAGO PRESS

CHICAGO AND LONDON

WALTER BERNS is the John M. Olin University Professor Emeritus at George-town University and resident scholar at the American Enterprise Institute. His books include *The First Amendment and the Future of American Democracy* (1976) and *Taking the Constitution Seriously* (1987).

The University of Chicago Press, Chicago 60637
The University of Chicago Press, Ltd., London
© 2001 by The University of Chicago
All rights reserved. Published 2001
Printed in the United States of America
10 09 08 07 06 05 04 03 02 01   1 2 3 4 5

ISBN: 0-226-04437-8 (cloth)

Library of Congress Cataloging-in-Publication Data

Berns, Walter, 1919–
    Making patriots / Walter Berns.
        p.   cm.
    Includes index.
    ISBN 0-226-04437-8 (cloth : alk. paper)
    1. Patriotism—United States—History. 2. Citizenship—United
States—History. 3. Political rights—United States—History.
4. Freedom of religion—United States—History. 5. Political
science—United States—History. I. Title.
JK1759 .B47   2001
320.54′09—dc21

                                                    00-011172

*To my
grandparents and great-grandparents
who immigrated to America*

CONTENTS

———•———

PREFACE

———·———

I belong to the generation of patriots that fought World War II. On the occasion of Winston Churchill's death in 1965, I wrote (in Cornell's student newspaper) that those who came after us could not fully understand why we, who remember the great and terrible events of 1940–41, should be so moved by his death; that they could not appreciate him as we did; that to them he was merely a name or, at most, a legendary figure, whereas to us he was, among other things, the embodiment of the greatest cause in our lives: the preservation of government of, by, and for the people at a time when it was most imperiled. We thought it altogether fitting and proper that (on April 9, 1963) he was made an honorary citizen of the United States.

Britain had, of course, been fighting for more than two years by the time we went to war, and it is not to belittle her contribution to final victory to say that the war could not have been won without us; Churchill knew this and acknowledged it. We were "the arsenal of democracy"; more than that, we were, as Abraham Lincoln said—not boastfully but as a fact—"the last, best hope of earth."

This was true in 1862 when Lincoln said it, as well as in 1941, and it is more obviously true today. Like it or not—and it *is* something of a burden, certainly a responsibility—America is to modern history as Rome was to ancient, and not only because we are the one remaining superpower. Modern politics began three hundred–plus years ago with the discovery or pronouncement of new principles, universal and revolutionary principles, respecting the rights of man. In 1776 we declared our right to form a new nation by appealing to these principles. Because we were the first to do so, it fell to us to be their champions, first by setting an example—this was Lincoln's point—and subsequently by defending them against their latter-day enemies, the Nazis and fascists in World War II and the communists in the cold war. Our lot is to be the one essential country, "the last, best hope of earth," and this ought to be acknowledged, beginning in our schools and universities, for it is only then that we can come to accept the responsibilities attending it.

Our unique place in the world is recognized elsewhere, sometimes grudgingly or inadvertently. In 1987, the bicentenary of our Constitution, I was in Brazil, where the people had recently overthrown a military dictatorship and had begun the process of writing a democratic constitution. I had been invited to lecture on constitutionalism. At one place, a university in Recife, after I had finished my prepared remarks, someone got up and denounced, not me, but the local official who had sponsored my appearance. "Why," he shouted, "did you invite an American? What can they tell us about constitutions? They've had only one. Why didn't you invite a Bolivian? They've had a hundred!"

I have enjoyed telling this story to students here, expecting them to appreciate it and hoping that they might even learn something from it. My hope is that they and their elders might learn something from this book, specifically, why this country deserves citizens who love and honor it, and are prepared to defend it.

Political scientist Sheldon Wolin had this in mind when he pointed out that we are citizens not only in the formal or legal sense, but because we share a birthright "inherited from our fathers," a birthright to be cared for, improved, and passed on to future generations.

ACKNOWLEDGMENTS

In 1997 Irving Kristol asked me to write an essay on patriotism for his journal, *The Public Interest;* this book is an outgrowth of that essay. In writing it, I have enjoyed the counsel of various friends and colleagues: Robert Bork, Werner J. Dannhauser, Hillel Fradkin, and Richard Stevens. My wife, reading it chapter by chapter, had to constantly remind me that I was not writing for an academic audience; I am grateful for this advice and have done my best to follow it. I am also grateful for the suggestions made by the two anonymous readers engaged by the University of Chicago Press. My greater debts, however, are to Kristol and to Robert Goldwin, both of whom read the entire manuscript and suggested how it might be improved, and to the American Enterprise Institute and its president, Christopher DeMuth. A "think tank," in Washington parlance, AEI provides a collegiate setting where scholars and others (including this retired professor) are able to study and write free of the constraints now imposed on universities by zealous public officials, and without having to worry about enrollments or, better yet, appointments, endowments, and budgets. De-Muth and his administrative colleagues take care of such matters. Finally, I would be remiss if I failed to acknowledge the assistance of various graduate students (chiefly Jeffry Morrison) who scoured the libraries for the books and other sources I needed.

INTRODUCTION

For what we can only presume to be good reasons, God willed that there be many nations, each with its own language (see Genesis 11:5–9) and, inevitably, its own interests. These interests not only differ but are also likely to come into conflict, which suggests that a patriot has to be more than a citizen or mere inhabitant of a nation; he has to be devoted to his nation and be prepared to defend it.

This was well understood in the nations (or cities) of classical antiquity, especially in Sparta, where the words "citizen" and "patriot" were essentially synonymous. Why this was so, or how this came to be so, is the subject of the first chapter of this book; here it is sufficient to point out that a Spartan had no interests other than the city's interests.

It is otherwise with Americans, a fact made evident in the case of Nathan Hale, arguably this country's most famous patriot. Hale said, as he was about to be executed by the British in 1776, "I only regret that I have but one life to lose for my country," and his alma mater, Yale, erected a statue of him on its Old Campus. "For God, for country, and for

Yale," as they say there, and, by saying it, they recognize that a patriot may have at least three interests and imply that he can be for all three, simultaneously and without reservation or equivocation.

This may be true at Yale (or may once have been true), but for most peoples, or, at least, for most Western peoples, patriotism has been something of a problem—not, of course, for the Spartans; their loyalties were not divided. A Spartan could be for Sparta without reservation or equivocation because there was nothing else in Sparta to be for: no gods, other than the city's gods, and no Yales, so to speak. This was not the case in that most famous of classical cities, Athens; like Sparta, Athens had its own gods, but, unlike Sparta, it had a sort of Yale, a community of academics with philosophic interests, one of whom (Socrates) it executed for his impiety and his allegedly corrupting effect on the youth of the city.

Patriotism became more of a problem with the advent of Christianity, which, by effecting a separation of the things that are Caesar's and the things that are God's, made it more likely that a person's loyalties would be divided. It became a still greater problem after Martin Luther. Where, before him, there had been one church in western Europe, there were soon to be many, as many churches as there were kingdoms; and in some of those kingdoms, there were many varieties of Christians. This was especially the case in the kingdom best known to Americans, the British. Could a Roman Catholic (Thomas More) obey his sovereign after his sovereign (Henry VIII) broke with Rome? Could the Scottish Presbyterians obey their king (Charles I), who ordered them to recognize the authority of Anglican bishops and to worship according to the Anglican Book of Common Prayer? Not likely, and, in the event, impossible: the pious More preferred the scaffold and the pious Scots, a civil war.

As I point out in the second chapter, our Founders were determined to avoid these old problems, and they succeeded, but only at the price of introducing a new one. Americans would not owe fealty to a monarch or a family, or be required to subscribe to an article of faith. They would pledge their allegiance to "the flag of the United States of America, and to the Republic for which it stands." The Republic, in turn, stands for a principle or idea, the idea first expressed by "the patriots of seventy-six" (as Lincoln called them), that all men are endowed by their Creator with certain "unalienable Rights," and that government is instituted "to secure these rights." This was new and was understood by the Founders to be new.

The late Martin Diamond had this in mind when, in an American government textbook, he points out that the terms "Americanism," "Americanization," and "un-American" have no counterparts in any other country or language. This is not by chance, or a matter of phonetics—Swissism? Englishization?—or mere habit. (What would a Frenchman have to do or believe in order to justify being labeled un-French?) The fact is, and it was first noted by the Englishman, G. K. Chesterton, the term "Americanism" reflects a unique phenomenon; as Diamond puts it, "It expresses the conviction that American life is uniquely founded on a set of political principles."*

The problem (the new one) arises from the fact that the Republic also stands for our country—our birthplace and

---

*Chesterton reports that when applying for a tourist visa, he was asked by an official in the American consulate whether he was an anarchist, and whether he was in favor of "subverting the government of the United States." He found this "funny" and "peculiar," but, on reflection, quite relevant and sensible. Americans can speak of "Americanism" and "Americanization" because, he says, America is founded on a creed and "is the only nation in the world that is founded on a creed" (G. K. Chesterton, *What I Saw in America* [New York: Dodd, Mead & Co., 1922], pp. 4, 7, 14).

the mansion of our fathers, as Alexis de Tocqueville put it—
and country and idea (or principle) are not necessarily con-
gruent; in fact, as we know very well, they can come into
conflict. Who was the patriot in the 1860s, Ulysses S. Grant
or Robert E. Lee? Opposed to slavery, Lee was tormented
by the necessity of having to choose between principle (the
natural equality of all men) and country, which for him
meant Virginia. In the end, he declined the offer of command of the Union army and went with Virginia, saying
that he could not raise his hand against his birthplace, his
home, and his children. Are we expected to think less of him
for this? Perhaps, but Grant did not; as I shall have occasion
to point out in chapter 5, he came to Lee's defense at a criti-
cal juncture after the war. (On the other hand, a number of
prominent southerners—e.g., Admiral David Farragut and
General George Thomas—stayed with and fought for the
Union, thereby testifying to the power of the Founders' design.)

   The twofold nature of American patriotism was well expressed by Lincoln in his eulogy on Henry Clay. Clay, he
said, was a patriot who "loved his country partly because it
was his own country, but mostly because it was a free country; and he burned with a zeal for its advancement, prosperity and glory, because he saw in such, the advancement,
prosperity and glory, of human liberty, human right and
human nature." As they were for Clay, country and principle
were one and the same for Lincoln, and his determination to
keep them the same, while preserving the integrity of the
principle, led him to fight the Civil War.

   It proved to be the deadliest of our wars, but it was also
the most necessary: at stake was the meaning of the Declaration of Independence. Like Lincoln, the Confederates ap-
pealed to it, but they insisted that its principle respecting the

natural equality of all men did not apply to Negroes; worse, given their reading of the Declaration, the Confederates had no alternative but to say Negroes were not human beings. I shall have more to say about the Civil War and the race issue in chapters 5 and 6; here, I only want to emphasize that to allow the South to secede from the Union, and to recognize its *right* to secede, would render the principle meaningless. And other peoples, beginning with their rulers, would draw this conclusion. Lincoln had this in mind when he said America was "the last, best hope of earth."

There is nothing peculiarly American about the Declaration's principles. On the contrary, they are abstract and universal principles of political right, a product of political philosophy; any people might subscribe to them, and Thomas Jefferson expected that, in the course of time, every other people would do so.* Were that to happen, and if the character of a country were determined solely, or even mainly, by the philosophical principles on which it is founded, every country would be a liberal democracy and America would lose its distinctiveness and, along with it, any greater claim on the affections and loyalties of its people. Why (except for reasons having to do with the climate) should they prefer America to liberally democratic Canada? And if the rest of the world consists of nothing but allegedly peaceful liberal democracies (see chapter 3), why, except to lend some pomp to state funerals and other official ceremonial occasions, should there be soldiers and sailors—or, for that matter,

wrong

---

*Speaking of the Declaration of Independence on the eve of its fiftieth anniversary, Jefferson said, "May it be to the world, what I hope it will be, (to some parts sooner, to others later, but finally to all,) the signal of arousing men to burst the chains under which monkish ignorance and superstition had persuaded them to bind themselves, and to assume the blessings and security of self-government. . . . All eyes are open, or opening, to the rights of man" (Letter to Roger C. Weightman, June 24, 1826).

public-spirited citizens? Indeed, if they are all fundamentally alike, or, as Jefferson puts it, if "all eyes are [really]
opened, or opening, to the rights of man," why should the
world be divided into countries or, as God said when He
scattered them, nations?

As it happened, this question had been asked and an-
swered in Europe even before 1826, when Jefferson had
implicitly posed it in America. In Paris in 1789, he had
witnessed the beginning of the French Revolution and
approved of it; in fact, he had helped his old friend the
Marquis de Lafayette draft the early versions of the French
Declaration of the Rights of Man and of the Citizen. And
why not? By appealing to natural right, were the French not
doing what we Americans had done in 1776? Were their
principles not America's principles? In one respect, they
surely were, but in the French version they were understood
to justify actions that caused Jefferson eventually—his critics said belatedly—to change his mind about the Revolution. To say nothing more (but see chapter 2), the French
revolutionaries chopped off the head of *their* king.

Edmund Burke, that great Anglo-Irish statesman and
political theorist and a friend of the American Revolution,
was quick to see the significance of what was going on in
France. He referred to it as an "extraordinary convulsion, the
effect of which on France, and even on all Europe . . . is
difficult to conjecture." He understood that the French Revolution, a "revolution in sentiments, manners and moral
opinions," was something new, and something alarming,
especially because its principles appeared to be readily ex-
portable; and those abstract, scientific, and universal principles, if exported—and unleavened by the unique experience
or traditions of a country—would reduce not only the French
but the peoples of all Europe to "one homogeneous mass."

Something like the homogenization of Europe did in fact begin to happen, but the Revolution, and what a Frenchman of our own time (Pierre Manent) has called the enormous Napoleonic enterprise, "unleashed a contrary movement of particularization and national separation." In a word, the attempt to export those universal principles gave rise to the glorification of the nation, which is to say, to nationalism and a politics of ethnicity where what matters is blood, not political principle.

Clearly, and made clearer still by the disorder and wars that followed, revolutionary France could not be what Jefferson expected America to be, "a light unto the nations." Rather than proclaim the rights of man, the nations went their own way, with their particular memories, manners, morals, and culture. "I speak *for* Germans simply, *of* Germans simply," said the philosopher Johann Fichte in 1807, a sentiment repeated by many another European. Out of this, in time, came the Nazi and other forms of fascist tyranny. But the idea of worldwide revolution did not die; within a few years it was given new life, but in a new form, by Karl Marx and the communists. A new form but with similar results: like Napoleon's efforts to spread French universalism, the Marxist revolution led to tyranny.

Marx claimed to have discovered the laws by which human history is governed, which enabled him (he claimed) not only to understand the past but also to predict the future. According to Marx, nothing happens by chance. Thus, the communist revolution was predictable because it was historically inevitable. Just as feudalism was superseded by capitalism (or liberal democracy), so capitalism would be superseded—and, according to Marxists, in Russia *was* superseded—by socialism, and in due course the socialist state would wither away, and, in the words of Marx's collaborator,

Friedrich Engels, the realm of necessity would be replaced by the realm of freedom. Born in Europe in the nineteenth century, this idea, and the promise it conveyed, captured the imagination of millions of people around the world.

But the Soviet Union, the socialist state par excellence, did not wither away, and never showed any signs of withering away; it collapsed of its own contradictions. Moreover, and in flat contradiction of Marx's theory of history, socialism has now been superseded by capitalism, not only in Eastern Europe but (perhaps) in Russia and the other parts of what was the Soviet Union. Marxism, which depended on history, has been discredited by history, and so has the idea of a worldwide Marxist revolution. The only ideal remaining (except in the Muslim world) is liberal democracy on the American model, and this (as the Marxists were wont to say) is not by chance.

It was American patriotism that had much to do with defeat of the twentieth-century tyrannies, the Nazi in World War II and the communist in the cold war. And for this, we Americans can be proud, or, at a minimum, take some satisfaction. Ours is not a parochial patriotism; precisely because it comprises an attachment to principles that are universal, we cannot be indifferent to the welfare of others. To be indifferent, especially to the rights of others, would be un-American.

Thus, we had no trouble whatsoever thinking of the Chinese students of Tiananmen Square as our fellows, and not merely because they erected a Statue of Liberty fashioned after ours. We could see immediately that they shared our "aims, aspirations, and values," as someone put it, and just as immediately, that the Chinese government did not. We were able to see these things because we continue to believe— and because our government continues to make it easy to believe—that all men are endowed by nature's God with certain unalienable rights. Believing this is part of what it means to be an American, and it is the job of the public schools to teach this to the younger generation of citizens.

This was well understood by our earliest educators, among them Thomas Jefferson (see chapter 4). The making of patriots could not be left to chance.

———

The Englishman Samuel Johnson said back in the eighteenth century that "patriotism is the last refuge of scoundrels." We have our share of them; they bomb federal office buildings and claim patriotic motives for doing so. But we have also had our share of heroes, patriots whom we admire because they fought for this country—with its universal principles and its particular sentiments, manners, and memories— and, despite all the current talk about globalization, there is no reason to believe we will not need their likes in the future.

CLASSICAL PATRIOTISM, ESPECIALLY THE SPARTAN

A Spartan woman had five sons in the army and was awaiting news of the battle. A Helot arrives; trembling, she asks him for news. "Your five sons were killed." "Base slave, did I ask you that?" "We won the victory." The mother runs to the temple and gives thanks to the gods.

Rousseau, *Émile*, from Plutarch, *Sayings of Spartan Women*

It would be convenient to believe that citizens will be patriots, but, in fact, neither citizenship nor patriotism can be taken for granted, especially in a liberal democracy like the United States. In the traditional or Spartan sense, patriots are citizens who love their country simply because it is their country—because it is "their birthplace and the mansion of their fathers," as Alexis de Tocqueville puts it in his

Democracy in America. Citizenship and patriotism were one
and the same thing in Sparta; it was a kind of filial piety. But
America is no Sparta.

Citizenship has, first of all, a legal meaning for us. According to the Constitution (see section 1 of the Fourteenth
Amendment), a citizen is any person "born or naturalized in
the United States, and subject to the jurisdiction thereof."
But citizenship is, even for us, more than legal status and the
enjoyment of the "privileges or immunities" attached thereto;
in its larger sense, it is a sentiment or state of mind, an
awareness of sharing an identity with others to whom one is
related by nationality, if not by blood, a sense of belonging to
a community for which one bears some responsibility. In a
word, citizenship implies public-spiritedness, and it is in
this sense that it cannot be taken for granted; like patriotism, it has to be cultivated.

They have to be cultivated because no one is born loving
his country; such love is not natural, but has to be somehow
taught or acquired. A person may not even be born loving
himself—the authorities differ on this—but he soon enough
learns to do so, and, unless something is done about it, he
will continue to do so, and in a manner that makes a concern
for country and fellow countrymen—or anyone other than
himself—difficult if not impossible to have. The problem is
as old as politics and no country is exempt from having to
deal with it, but, for reasons having to do with our democratic principles, we cannot do so as others have before us.

To deal with it, Socrates, the first political philosopher,
proposed a comprehensive program of education for the
guardians of the city. As described by Plato (*Republic,* 414d-
e), this consisted of a carefully designed program in gym-
nastics (for the body) and music (for the soul). Socrates then
suggests that the guardians be told a tale; the tale is meant to

persuade them that it is natural for them to love and care for their city. They must be told that they only dreamed they had been educated in and by the city; that they were born of the earth and were fully formed, along with their weapons, while in it, and that the earth, "which is their mother," had then "sent them up," and that now, as though their land were their mother and nurse, "they must plan for it and defend it, and they must think of the other citizens as brothers and born of this [bit of] earth."

It is hard to believe that anyone, least of all an American, could credit this tale—Socrates himself calls it a lie—but it does serve to highlight this most fundamental of political problems. Besides, the Spartans seemed to believe it, or, to be more precise, something like it.

Although a city that had known a few traitors during its long history—the most notorious being Pausanias, the general who conspired with King Xerxes during the Greek war with Persia—still, it is not for nothing that the word "Spartan" has come to be understood as synonymous with "patriot." Every factor, demographic and geographic, and every detail of Spartan education contributed to public-spiritedness.

Spartans were a homogeneous people, descended from the same ancestors, few in number and inhabiting an area smaller than the District of Columbia; a people whose boys were trained, almost from the time of their birth, to be soldiers, to be courageous and obedient, to endure pain, heat, and cold, and, of course, to be adept in the martial arts; whose girls were required to exercise naked (in public), with a view to producing sons capable of being soldiers (and daughters capable of breeding them); and whose infants, if they chanced to be puny or ill-formed, were exposed in a chasm (the *Apothetae*) and left to die; a people who were not supposed to know the meaning of privacy, who took their meals at common public tables, eating the same bread and meat, simple and healthy fare, and all the while being instructed in public affairs; a people whose law allowed them, indeed encouraged them, to kill their Helots, their slaves who rather resembled but, because they were not of the same Dorian race, were said to be not like them, and were a danger to them because they greatly outnumbered them; a people whose legendary lawgiver (Lycurgus), in an effort to do away with arrogance, envy, luxury, and avarice, ordered the confiscation of all gold and silver coins, replacing them with iron coins of great weight and little face value, thereby hoping to discourage the accumulation of wealth (because, as Plutarch says, to lay up an amount of considerable value would require "a pretty large closet, and, to remove it, nothing less than a yoke of oxen"), a currency that put an end to foreign trade and the importation of foreign luxuries (because the iron coins would not be accepted as legal tender by any other Greek city); a city whose few poets—only classical scholars can come up with their names—wrote mainly of wars and warriors; and, finally, a city that discouraged what would seem to be the natural human tendency to raise questions about right and wrong, or, as Plato's Athenian Stranger puts it, "that does not allow any of the young to inquire which laws are finely made and which are not, but that commands all to say in harmony, in one voice from one mouth, that all the laws are finely made by the gods."

Athens produced philosophers (Socrates, Plato), historians (Thucydides), playwrights (Aristophanes, Sophocles), sculptors (Phidias), and world-famous statesmen (Pericles); Sparta, a city that existed for upwards of five hundred years, produced (so far as most of us know) only Leonidas and the three hundred who fought and died at Thermopylae, patriots who loved their city more than they loved themselves, who saw themselves, and were seen by each other, as nothing but citizen-soldiers, who had no existence except as citizen-soldiers. As a modern commentator on the Spartan regime rightly says, "The subordination of the individual to the state has had no parallel in the history of the world."

Still, Sparta has had its admirers, even in the modern world; Jean-Jacques Rousseau spoke well of it, and Samuel Adams once hoped to build a "Christian Sparta" in America. But nothing came of that, and nothing could have come of it. Sparta, a city that discouraged self-interest and self-gratification, could not possibly provide a model for America. But, then, neither could any other classical republic, not even Athens.

Admittedly, Athens was a city unlike Sparta, and Pericles, in his famous Funeral Oration, makes much of the differences between them. Although he was speaking in the first year of the Peloponnesian War (430 B.C.), Pericles points out that Athenian youth, unlike those of their enemy Sparta, were not subjected to a painful military discipline almost from the time of their birth, nor were their elders simply soldiers. Athenians lived exactly as they pleased, he says, engaging in private industry, enjoying private pleasures and luxuries from abroad, as well as those of their own making. Compared with Sparta, which did not welcome foreigners, Athens was an open as well as a self-governing society. Not only did Athenians enjoy free government, but this freedom extended to their "ordinary lives"; for example, as Pericles says, neighbors did not exercise a "jealous surveillance" over each other—which is to say, they did not spy on each other.

On the other hand, and despite our practice of celebrating it as the birthplace of democracy and the nursery of Western civilization, Athens was not like America, either.

Pericles makes that clear as well. He says Athenians were "lovers of wisdom," which suggests that their constitution, like ours, protected freedom of speech and freedom of religion, but, after what amounted to a fair trial, they executed Socrates for his impiety; there was no separation of church and state in Athens. Nor was there anything resembling what we call "civil society" or "mediating structures," the sort of private associations that Tocqueville remarked on his visit to America. There were, instead, only the people and the city, and nothing in between. True, the people lived in households, but by the time of Pericles these households had lost whatever independence they might once have enjoyed. Originally, each worshiped its own ancestors at its own household altars, but in time the household was extended until it became the village, then the city; and Athens, like every other Greek city, had its own gods. Just as there was no separation of church and state, so there was no separation of state and religion, or, as we might say, no division between the spiritual and the temporal. Furthermore, not only were Athenians expected to prefer public duty to private pleasure, but, according to Pericles, they were enjoined to love the city, in fact, to be "lovers" (*erastai*) of their city.

This, surely, is an extraordinary injunction. How could it possibly be obeyed? After all, and with good reason, we think of eros as the most private of passions, the passion, when it is reciprocated, that joins lover to beloved—Antony to Cleopatra, Romeo to Juliet, Anna Karenina to Count Vronsky, which meant, in these cases, the passion that led Antony to forsake his city, Rome, for Cleopatra, Romeo and Juliet to forsake their families for each other, and Anna to forsake husband and child for Vronsky. Yet Pericles treats it as a passion capable of joining citizen to city, of causing him not only to give his life for the city, but also to find his fulfillment in and through the city, or to forget himself in the city. One might well wonder whether even Pericles thought this possible.

Pericles says Athenians were lovers of beauty, and Athens was indeed a beautiful city. (Pericles was personally responsible for much of this beauty, including, among other public buildings, the Parthenon on the Acropolis, "one of the brightest jewels in mankind's treasury.") But it was not its beauty, rather it was its military power, and the empire gained by means of that power, that was said to make it lovable. Its power was such that Sparta feared it, Corinth envied it, most of the Aegean cities submitted to it, and its citizens gloried in it. Its colonies (or allies) extended from Byzantium (modern-day Istanbul) in the north to Rhodes in the south, from the coastal cities of Asia Minor in the east to the coast of Sicily in the west. Athenians were enjoined to be lovers of Athens because they *were* Athens—in a way, by loving their city, they loved themselves—and because, by gaining an empire, Athens provided them with the means by which they gained fame and glory. And according to Pericles, glory is what human beings want above everything else. As Clifford Orwin writes (by way of explaining what Pericles had in mind), "Only through the empire does the city achieve such a peak of splendor that the citizens yearn from the heart of their being for apotheosis in and through it."

The connection between war and patriotism, or better, between war and the making of patriots, is evident; perhaps even self-evident. Athens needed patriotic citizens in order to make war, and, although Pericles insists that it was fighting the Peloponnesian War out of necessity, by making war it had gained the empire that fulfilled the spiritual needs of its citizens. Sparta, too, needed patriotic citizens, but only to defend Greece against Persia and itself against the likes of Athens; still, although it harbored no imperial ambitions, Sparta was no less warlike. The institutions of both Athens and Sparta were ordered with a view to war and, precisely for this reason, neither Athens nor Sparta could, or can, provide a model for America. America is a republic, but not a republic like Athens or Sparta.

Alexander Hamilton had this in mind when he says in *Federalist* 8 that "the industrious habits of the people of the present day, absorbed in the pursuits of gain and devoted to the improvements of agriculture and commerce, are incompatible with the condition of a nation of soldiers, which was the true condition of the people of those [ancient Greek] republics." But it is not only our industrious and other private habits that distinguish us from Spartans, Athenians, Corinthians, and the rest; there is also the size and composition of our population. We are not few but many—even in our beginning our numbers were many times those of any of the Greek cities—and we are no longer, if we ever were, a people descended from the same ancestors. We claimed to have declared our independence as "one people," but we now take pleasure in our "diversity," which, leaving aside 1776, has something to do with the fact that we have always had difficulty acting as one united people, even when fighting a war. In principle, whereas no stranger could become a Spartan, and only a minority of the residents of Athens were Athenian citizens, anybody can become an American, and millions of people from around the world have done so, which helps to explain why that patriotic word "fatherland" has no place in our vocabulary.

But nothing distinguishes us so sharply from the classical republics, or bears more directly on the issue of citizenship, than the principles governing our birth as a nation and then incorporated in the Republic we ordained and established. These principles gave rise to an altogether new understanding of what it means to be a patriotic citizen. To paraphrase a line from Abraham Lincoln's 1862 message to Congress, our case was new, so we had to think and act anew. What he thought, and how he acted, is the subject of a later chapter in this book.

Here it is appropriate to say a few words about the newness of "our case," or, to recall the motto inscribed on the Great Seal of the United States (and reproduced on every dollar bill), what it is that made for a *novus ordo seclorum,* which is to say, a new order of the ages. We were the first nation to declare its independence by appealing not to the past but to the newly discovered "Laws of Nature and of Nature's God," and this had (and has) consequences for patriotism. Whereas the God of Abraham, Isaac, and Jacob imposed duties on all men (see Exodus 20:1–17), "Nature's God" endowed all men with rights; and, whereas the God of the New Testament commanded all men to love God and their neighbors as themselves (see Matthew 22:37–40), nature's God created a state of nature in which everyone was expected to take care of himself and, as "America's philosopher" said (see John Locke, *Treatises* II, sec. 6), take care of others only "when his own preservation comes not in competition." And so long as he remains in the state of nature, he has the right to do what he is naturally inclined to do, and what he is naturally inclined to do is not to take care of others. To say the least, he is not naturally inclined to be a patriotic citizen.

In fact, he is not *naturally* inclined to be a citizen of any sort. Endowed by nature with certain private rights, he enters civil society, and then agrees to be governed, but only in order to secure those private rights. He is a far cry from the

Athenian described by Pericles; glory and empire mean nothing to him. His aspiration is to lead an essentially private life, joining, but only if he so wishes, one or another of the private associations constituting what has come to be called civil society: a church, a labor union, a trade association, a club, or whatever. He asks of government only that it protect his rights, and (except in times of crisis) the government, besides asking him to respect the rights of others, asks very little of him in return. He is expected to perform his civic duties, of course, but he is not required to do so; for example, he is not required to vote or hold public office. He lives in a self-governing democracy, but, unlike the citizens of every previously existing democracy, he, himself, does not govern. Governing is done by his representatives.

It is, of course, true that he is required to surrender his natural rights when leaving the state of nature—except, of course, the few unalienable ones, the surrender of which would contradict the very purpose of the flight from nature—but in exchange, as it were, he gains the security that only government can provide. For example, the Constitution makes it clear that he cannot be deprived of life, liberty, and property without "due process of law." As John Jay says in *Federalist* 2, "Nothing is more certain than the indispensable necessity of government; and it is equally undeniable that whenever and however it is instituted, the people must cede to it some of their natural rights, in order to vest it with requisite powers." Nevertheless, it remains true with us that rights are primary and duties are secondary and derivative. Designing a public-spirit curriculum for such a people is no easy task.

Of course, when properly understood, the Declaration is not merely a catechism of individual rights. In fact, it claims to be the act, not of isolated individuals, but of "one people," a people with the "Right" to abolish one government and to "institute" another, and an entity in which individuals are bound to each other, contractually if not naturally. Accordingly, it was signed by men who pledged to each other their lives, their fortunes, and their sacred honor. Except hypocritically, and the Founders were not hypocrites, such a pledge cannot be made by selfish or simply self-interested individuals. Yet, on the face of the document, the rights are inherent, whereas the duties have to be acquired.

The Founders were aware of the problem posed by this. They feared that we would claim our rights, and even, as has proved to be the case, that we would convert many an interest into a right, and all the while neglecting our duties. That is why James Madison and his Federalist colleagues resisted the demand made by Patrick Henry and other Anti-Federalists that a bill of natural rights, similar to that in the Virginia Declaration of Rights, be affixed to the Constitution, indeed, be attached to it as a preamble. Having established a free government—no simple task—they saw the necessity of citizens willing to support it, even to fight for it, and feared that such support would be jeopardized by giving rights, especially natural rights, pride of place in the Constitution.

Herbert Storing made their point in our own time with a couple of questions. "Does a constant emphasis on unalienable natural rights foster good citizenship or a sense of community?" he asks. "Does a constant emphasis on the right to abolish government foster the kind of popular support that any government needs?" As Storing says, the Federalists— led here by Madison—did not doubt that these first principles were true, that they may be resorted to under circumstances similar to those of 1776, and that they provided the ultimate source and justification of government. Their point was that even a rational and well-constituted government needs and deserves a presumption of legitimacy and permanence, and, to quote Storing again, "a bill of rights that presses these first principles to the fore tends to deprive government of that presumption." Patrick Henry disagreed, and, of greater consequence, so did Jefferson.

Jefferson believed that the people had to be regularly reminded of first principles.* In addition to agreeing with Henry on the need of a bill of rights, including natural rights, he advocated frequent conventions of the people for the purpose of altering the Constitution or "correcting breaches of it." Again, Madison acknowledged that this plan was "strictly consonant to republican theory," as he puts it in *Federalist* 49, but he was, nevertheless, strongly opposed to it. He objected, he writes, because every appeal to the people would carry an implication of some defect in the government, and "frequent appeals would, in great measure, deprive the government of that veneration which time bestows on everything, and without which perhaps the wisest and freest government would not possess the requisite stability." Madison granted that citizens ought to revere the laws, and that, in a nation of Jeffersons, this reverence could be inculcated by the voice of an enlightened reason. But such a nation, he says, "is as little to be expected as the philosophical race of kings wished for by Plato [and] in every other nation, the most rational government will not find it a

---

*With this in mind, Jefferson called for occasional if not frequent rebellions. As he put it in a letter from Paris in November 1787, "The tree of liberty must be refreshed from time to time with the blood of patriots and tyrants."

These words have made Jefferson something of a hero among our self-styled "patriots." Timothy McVeigh, for example, was wearing a T-shirt with these words on it when he was arrested after blowing up the federal office building in Oklahoma City, killing 168 patriots (or, at any rate, citizens) and no tyrants, and his friend Terry Lynn Nichols is said to have also been inspired by them.

superfluous advantage to have the prejudices of the community on its side." As I shall argue in the fifth chapter of this book, Lincoln, our greatest teacher of what it means to be an American, reached a similar conclusion.

Finally, on this subject of our newness, we differ from the likes of Sparta and Athens not only in our public principles, but in our private beliefs, and our public principles require the government to respect private beliefs, especially religious beliefs. This can give rise to a problem because America was settled largely by Christians and, even today, is inhabited largely by Christians, and Christians are enjoined, indeed, commanded, to love God before their country.

GOD BEFORE COUNTRY?

The victory of Christianity marks the end of ancient society. . . . The idea
which men had of the duties of the citizen [was] modified. The first duty no
longer consisted in giving one's time, one's strength, one's life to the state. Politics
and war were no longer the whole of man; all the virtues were no longer com-
prised in patriotism, for the soul no longer had a country. Man felt that he had
other obligations besides that of living and dying for the city. Christianity distinguished the private from the public virtues. By giving less honor to the latter, it
elevated the former; it placed God, the family, the human individual above
country, the neighbor above city.

Fustel de Coulanges, *The Ancient City*

The statement quoted in the epigraph above comes from
the concluding chapter of the author's celebrated study
of the religion, laws, and institutions of Greece and Rome.
One might think it obvious that a Frenchman, and more to
the point a European, should think of the postclassical
world as a Christian world. But he spoke of Christianity not
only because his world was Christian, but because, alone

among the monotheistic religions, Christianity—not Juda-ism, not Islam—effected a separation, not of church and state (that comes later), but of the temporal and the spiritual, or, as Jesus put it, between the things that are Caesar's and the things that are God's.

To appreciate the significance of this, particularly its effect on citizenship in western Europe, one can begin by recalling Pericles' praise of Athens. As he says, Athenians were supposed to be "lovers" of their city, which meant to be committed to it body and soul; and everything in Athens—all the statues, temples, spectacles, or religious ceremonies—gave evidence of that single commitment. Athenians were not divided in their loyalties. But by separating the spiritual from the temporal, Jesus not only provided the basis for the subsequent separation of church and state, but, even before the advent of the liberal state, he made it impossible for a Christian to be a patriotic citizen in the classical sense. From this time forward, Athenians and all other Europeans would have two masters—one civil, the other ecclesiastical—and, to quote Jean-Jacques Rousseau (who, of course, was speaking before the advent of the United States), "no people has ever been able to figure out whom it was obliged to obey, the ruler or the priest."

Unity was not regained, or the difficulty resolved, by making Christianity the official religion of the state and anointing a king to rule it, as David was anointed king over the house of Judah. This did not prevent a king from disagreeing with a priest, or a priest with a king, and sometimes with fatal consequences (Thomas à Becket with Henry II; Thomas More with Henry VIII). And just as kings could quarrel with priests, and priests with kings, so priests could quarrel with each other over Christian doctrine, and these quarrels could have political consequences. For example, the pope in Rome and the various patriarchs in the East, all Catholics, could quarrel over whether the Holy Spirit proceeds from the Father alone (the position of what became the Orthodox Church) or (the position of Rome) from the Father and the Son together. This so-called *filioque* dispute began in the fourth century and culminated seven hundred years later when, in the year 1054, Pope Leo IX excommunicated the patriarch in Constantinople, Michael Cerularius, and the entire Eastern Church, and, as a result, provided the ground of the dispute between the Croats and Serbs, who, when not governed by an emperor or a dictator (Tito), have been killing each other ever since.

Of greater consequence for Europe was the dispute, five hundred years later, between Rome and Martin Luther, a dispute that ended by destroying the unity of Western Christendom. An Augustinian friar and German priest, Luther began by accusing the Church of corruption and went on to challenge the pope over such matters as the selling of indulgences, his presumed authority over secular rulers, the finality of his interpretation of Scripture, and the right of priests, as "shepherds of souls," to mediate between the laity and God. Threatened with excommunication, Luther said, or is alleged to have said, "Here I stand. I can do no other. God help me. Amen." His appeal to conscience set an example that others would follow. Should the pious Scot obey his king or his Presbyterian conscience? That question was posed in seventeenth-century Britain when King Charles I ordered the Scots to worship according to the Anglican Book of Common Prayer and acknowledge the authority of its episcopacy; the Scots' refusal provoked a half-century of civil war and revolution.

Jesus envisioned many kingdoms and one church, but after the Reformation there were as many churches as there were kingdoms, and in some kingdoms, among them the British, one established church but many varieties of Christians: Catholics, Puritans, Quakers, Presbyterians, as well as Anglicans. Charles claimed to exercise both "Spirituall and Temporall" powers, but only the Anglicans acknowledged his claim; rather than recognize his right to prescribe the terms or forms of their worship, the Puritans fled to the Continent, then to America; the Quakers suffered imprisonment; and the Catholics went underground, worshiping in secret. As for the obstinate Scots, they entered into a covenant and, under its banner, formed an army that fought on the parliamentary side in the civil war, at the end of which the king lost his head, literally, as did the archbishop of Canterbury, William Laud.

They were all Christians: Laud as well as Oliver Cromwell; the Earl of Strafford as well as the parliamentarians who impeached and executed him for treason; George Jeffreys, the judge who presided over the "Bloody Assizes" of 1685, as well as Richard Rumbold, whose words, spoken on the scaffold, were later quoted by Thomas Jefferson. All Christians, all patriots willing to give their lives for their country, but unable to agree as to who was authorized to speak for that country. Two powers, two sovereigns, and a never-ending dispute over jurisdiction—there was much in this history to confirm Rousseau's judgment that a sound constitution was impossible in a Christian state.

The political philosopher Thomas Hobbes—a contemporary of Laud, Strafford, Cromwell, and the rest—had come to the same conclusion. As Rousseau says, Hobbes was "the only Christian writer" clearly to perceive both the evil and the remedy, namely, that "the two heads of the eagle be reunited, *i.e.*, that everything *else* be subordinated to political unity—in the absence of which there will never be a well-constituted state or government." What Hobbes failed to see (according to Rousseau) was that "Christianity, given its domineering cast of mind, could not keep house with the system he advocated, and that the interest of the priest would in the long run prevail over the interest of the state." Rousseau met this problem (if problem it was) by proposing that the state replace Christianity with a religion without priests, a "civil religion" (the title of the chapter in his *Social Contract* from which I have been quoting).

Rousseau was to have a profound effect in Europe, and, in subtle ways, even in America—for example, and I shall turn to this subject in the next chapter, he invented the "bourgeois," the phenomenon or human type despised by artists and intellectuals—but, in declaring our independence and writing our Constitution, our Founders took their bearings from another "Christian writer," John Locke.

Strangely (because he was thoroughly familiar with his work), Rousseau makes no mention here of Locke, who also perceived the evil, but, unlike Hobbes, proposes what proved to be an effective remedy, particularly in America. Locke himself was a victim of the day's religious intolerance and, to escape it and to reduce the risk of his ending up on the gallows with his friend Richard Rumbold, he left England for the Continent. There, and more precisely in Utrecht, he employed himself in writing his celebrated *Letter Concerning Toleration,* which was destined to have a profound influence in America. Jefferson, for example, had not only read the *Letter,* but had taken careful notes on it, and these notes, bearing Locke's teaching, found their way into the Virginia Statute for Religious Freedom.* (Harvard his-

---

*Jefferson goes further than Locke, who, probably because he thought it would be fruitless at the time, did not propose the toleration of Roman Catholics and atheists.

torian Bernard Bailyn, no mean authority on such matters, goes so far as to say that this statute is the "most important document in American history, bar none.") As is evident in his draft of the Virginia Statute, Jefferson understood very well that, despite the title he gave to his *Letter,* what Locke proposed was not toleration but the separation of church and state, a policy based on an altogether different principle, and a policy designed to solve the problem of divided loyalties.

To tolerate means to allow, to permit, to put up with, as we say; it derives from the Latin *tolero,* meaning to bear or endure. This meaning was embodied in the Toleration Act of 1689, which the English historian Thomas Babington Macaulay praises as "very near to the idea of a great English law." That act did not divest the Church of England of its formal authority; it did not in any way cast doubt on the validity of the Church's Thirty-nine Articles of Religion or renounce the state's right to punish anyone who refused to subscribe to them. As Macaulay writes, "The Toleration Act recognized persecution as the rule, and granted liberty of conscience only as the exception." But Locke claims, "Liberty of conscience is every man's natural right," a statement echoed by Jefferson in the Virginia Statute, where we read that "the rights hereby asserted are of the natural rights of mankind," and echoed again in his *Notes on the State of Virginia.* To secure those rights, Locke proposed, and America adopted, the policy of separating church and state, a policy based on the natural right of conscience.

The best statement of the American policy can be found in George Washington's response to the address from the Hebrew Congregation of Newport, Rhode Island:

It is now no more that tolerance is spoken of, as if it was by the indulgence of one class of people, that another enjoyed the exercise of

their inherent natural rights, for, happily, the government of the
United States, which gives to bigotry no sanction, to persecution
no assistance, requires only that they who live under its protec-
tion should demean themselves as good citizens, in giving it on
all occasions their effectual support. . . . May the children of the
Stock of Abraham who dwell in this land continue to merit and
enjoy the good will of the other inhabitants—while everyone
shall sit in safety under his own vine and fig tree and there shall
be none to make him afraid.

The dispensation described here by Washington was a far
cry from that in England, even after the Toleration Act of
1689. That act was of great benefit to certain Protestant dissenters, who, as Macaulay writes, were "permitted by law to
worship God according to their own conscience." They
were forbidden to meet behind barred doors, but at the same
time they were protected against hostile intrusion. The
Quakers, in turn, were not required to sign any of the
Church of England's Thirty-nine Articles of Religion, but
the benefits of the act were extended to them nevertheless;
they had only to make a general statement of faith accompanied by a sort of pledge of allegiance to King William and
Queen Mary—and, as well, a declaration of their abhor-
rence of that "damnable Doctrine and Position that Princes
Excommunicated or Deprived by the Pope or any Authority
of the See of Rome may be Deposed or Murthered by their
Subjects or any other whatsoever." In practice, if not all that
clearly, certain Protestant worshipers were tolerated; in
practice, and very clearly, Roman Catholics—to say nothing of "Jews, Turks, and Infidels"—were not. Catholics and
the non-Christians would fare better—but, as the Chinese
especially learned, not always well—in America.

Rousseau, an admirer of the unity that prevailed in the

classical city, proposed to regain a semblance of it and, thereby, resolve this problem of divided loyalties once and for all, by abolishing the Christian state, as it existed, in favor of a republic like that of classical Athens, Sparta, or Rome, a republic with "its own religion and its own gods," as he puts it. Locke, in turn, proposed to restore unity by taking religion out of politics, by consigning it, and thereby (he hoped) confining it, to the private sphere, where each member of society is free to worship (or not worship) as he pleases.

Locke's formula for unity amounted to this: religion would have no state, and the state would have no religion. A religion without a state (i.e., without a state to support it) will inevitably be one among many religions, all equal in the eyes of the law, and each required not only to live at peace with the others but to recognize the right of the others to preach, teach, and proselytize. This was obviously impossible in England with its established church, but, thanks to Locke and his followers here (Washington, but especially Madison and Jefferson), it quickly became a reality in America. Alexis de Tocqueville took note of this in the 1830s. As he wrote to his friend Louis de Kergolay back in France, "Go into the churches (I mean the Protestant ones), you will hear morality preached, of dogma not a word. Nothing that can at all shock the neighbor; nothing that can arouse the idea of dissent."

A state without religion is a state of limited powers; unlike the classical republics, and unlike even England after the Toleration Act, its business has to do only with the things of this world, not of the world to come, which is to say, with the protection of the life, liberty, and property of its people, not with the care of their souls. As Locke writes, "The care . . . of every man's soul belongs unto himself, and is to be left unto himself." Liberty of conscience, in Jefferson's words, is one of "the natural rights of mankind," one of the rights we invoked when declaring our independence in 1776 and, in 1789, given constitutional status in the religious provisions of the First Amendment: "Congress shall make no law respecting an establishment of religion, or *prohibiting the free exercise thereof . . .*" (emphasis added).

This provision is frequently quoted, but an important aspect of it is seldom noted: with the free exercise of one's religion comes the requirement to obey the law regardless of one's religious beliefs.* The freedom (to worship) and the requirement (to obey the law) come together, connected by the principle from which they both derive: the separation of church and state, or of the private and the public, specifically of religious belief and the law, with the understanding that, when they conflict, the law prevails and must be obeyed. A severe command, perhaps, but obeying it brings a considerable benefit. As Locke writes, by excluding all private judgments, "the community comes to be [governed] by settled standing rules, indifferent and the same to all parties, and by men having authority from the community for the execution of those rules" (*Treatises* II, sec. 87). Whether a law is just or unjust is a judgment that belongs to no "private man," however pious or learned or, as we say today, sincere he may be. This means that we are first of all citizens, and only secondarily Christians, Jews, Muslims, or of any other religious persuasion.

Not everyone agrees with my account of our founding principles, some because they believe I am mistaken about Locke's teaching or his influence in America, others simply

---

*Washington had this in mind when, in his response to the Hebrew Congregation of Newport, he said that citizens are required to give the government their effectual support "on all occasions" (see above, p. 29).

because they refuse to believe that America is, in principle, a secular state. Instead, they insist, as a Supreme Court justice once flatly stated, that America is "a Christian nation," and in support of this judgment refer to the Declaration of Independence.

But the God invoked there is "Nature's God," not, or arguably not, the God of the Bible, not the God whom, today, 43 percent of Americans (a number far exceeding that in any of the other Western democracies) claim regularly to worship on the Sabbath. Nature's God issues no commandments, no one can fall from his grace, and, therefore, no one has reason to pray to him asking for his forgiveness; he makes no promises. On the contrary, he endowed us with "certain unalienable Rights," then left us alone, and with the knowledge, or at least the confidence, that he will never interfere in our affairs. Moreover, he is not a jealous god; he allows us—in fact, he endows us with the right—to worship other gods or even no god at all. This right can best be secured—Jefferson, Madison, and the others insisted it could *only* be secured—under secular auspices, under a government that takes no stand on matters of faith.

Here one can see the extent of Locke's influence in America. Liberty of conscience—based on his principle that the care "of every man's soul belongs unto himself, and is to be left unto himself"—became part of the law, federal and eventually state. As a consequence, America became what no other country had ever been (and what the Episcopal Church can only claim to be): a haven "for all sorts and conditions of men," not only for Christians of every variety, but also, to use the term of art, for "Jews, Turks, and Infidels," as well.

Liberty of conscience was widely accepted at the time of the Founding, but this did not prevent some jurists and legislators from insisting, at least for a while (and given our principles it could be only for a while), that Christianity was part of the law, meaning the common law. So it had been in England, and so, it was assumed by some (but not by Jefferson), it would continue to be in America. But there was no disagreement about the place of the common law. Indeed, one of the first things done by the states after independence was to declare (here in the words of the New Jersey constitution of 1776) that "the common law of England, as well as so much of the statute law, as have been heretofore practiced in this Colony, shall remain in force, until they shall be altered by a future law of the Legislature; such parts only excepted, as are repugnant to the rights and privileges contained in this Charter [or constitution]."

But if the "rights and privileges" contained in the various state charters or constitutions included the right of liberty of conscience, and if, in turn, this right required, in Madison's words, "a perfect separation between ecclesiastical and civil matters," what did it mean to say that Christianity was part of the common law? Very little, as it turned out; and it turned out as it had to turn out. Consider, for example, the case of blasphemy in America. It was and remained a crime under the common law, and the states punished it as they had done when they were colonies, and continued to do so until 1921—but only by redefining the offense.

This was done in the first case tried after independence. In 1811 the New York Supreme Court held that blasphemy, contrary to the English and colonial courts, was an offense not against God, but, rather, against the community. A Delaware court reached the same conclusion in 1837. The Delaware defendant, named Thomas Jefferson Chandler, was charged with uttering an unlawful, wicked, and blasphemous attack on the Christian religion, insofar as he did pronounce, in a loud voice and "in the presence and hearing of diverse citizens of [the] state . . . *that the virgin Mary was a whore and Jesus Christ a bastard.*" Chandler admitted the utterance—he was in no position to deny it—but protested his innocence by citing certain letters written by his famous namesake; the court found him guilty, nevertheless. It agreed that Christianity was part of the common law, and that blasphemy was a crime under that law, but only because blasphemy was likely to cause a breach of the peace. This was not, said the court, a matter of protecting Christianity or any of its precepts; rather, it was merely a matter of taking judicial cognizance of the fact that Delaware was inhabited largely by Christians, and that the blasphemy in question was an attack on their faith. Alter these facts, and the result would have been the same. Suppose, the court said, the people of Delaware were to "repudiate the religion of their fathers" and adopt Judaism or Islam; it would then be a crime to revile the name of Moses or the prophet Muhammad. "Will any man say that the public vengeance would not probably break out in open acts of violence against the author of such insults, especially were it once understood that there exists no law to punish him?"

In the course of his opinion, the chief justice of the Delaware court referred to an 1824 Pennsylvania case where the court, by way of justifying its judgment upholding the conviction, said it was essential for the law to punish blasphemous utterances. "It is liberty run mad, to declaim against the punishment of these offenses, or to assert that the punishment is hostile to the spirit and genius of our government." Without these restraints, said the court, "no free government could long exist." True, perhaps, but the court might have gone on to say, and this time without exaggerating, that the law of blasphemy was hostile to the spirit and genius of American government. Rather than declaring it unconstitutional as a denial of the rights of conscience, these early state courts stripped blasphemy of its religious character, making it an offense against the state rather than against the Christian (or any other) church. Judges in a liberal state, they had no other alternative. The citizens of this liberal state were divided by religion, and the condition of their being politically united is a government that does not favor a particular religion. Americans learned this from Locke.

A cursory reading of Locke's *Letter Concerning Toleration* would lead one to believe that his purpose was to get the state off the backs of the churches, but, as Jefferson understood very well, his chief purpose was to get the churches off the back of the state and thereby, in the words of our Constitution, "insure domestic Tranquility." In Locke's own words, "It is not the diversity of opinions (which cannot be avoided), but the refusal of toleration to those that are of different opinions . . . that has produced all the bustles and wars that have been in the Christian world upon account of religion." With religion taken out of politics, the religious would have no reason to engage in political quarrels with each other—who can quarrel over a blasphemy law that protects one and all alike?—or, on religious grounds, to challenge the authority of a liberal state.

This was not an unreasonable expectation because (to seize again upon that phrase from the Episcopal Book of Common Prayer), the liberal state would offer protection to "all sorts and conditions of men." To say nothing further about blasphemy, it would not ban its Catholics or inhibit their worship, banish its Jews, imprison its Quakers, coerce its Presbyterians, put a price on the head of its Salman Rushdies, or prohibit anyone, because of his faith, from holding public office. It would be a state to which all men, at least all "reasonable" men, could pledge their allegiance, and without reservation. In a word, they could be patriotic citizens, disposed to obey the laws because, being enacted by a state without religion, the laws would be less likely to offend their religious precepts or sensibilities: less likely, but not always unlikely even in America.

America guarantees liberty of conscience and, as a result, now finds itself with some fifteen hundred different religious sects or organizations, some of them with bizarre precepts and practices, practices that are certain to be contrary to seemingly "neutral" laws. Thus, the Amish were "offended" by a law requiring their children to attend school (they won in the Supreme Court); the Santerians by a law forbidding the ritual killing of animals, chickens in their case (they, too, won in the Supreme Court); the Indians of the Native American Church by a law forbidding the use of hallucinogenic drugs (they lost in the Supreme Court, then won in Congress); the Sikhs by a law forbidding children to carry daggers to school (they won, so long as the daggers were sheathed); and the religious pacifists by the laws requiring military service.

The subject of conscientious objection has a long history in this country and deserves more than a cursory reference. As early as 1775, the Continental Congress adopted a resolution recognizing, and advising the various colonies to recognize, that there are people (originally the Quakers, Mennonites, and Schwenkfelders) whose religious principles forbid them to "bear arms in any case," and the Congress went on to make it clear that it intended "no violence to their consciences." It did, however, urge them to serve their "distressed brethren in the several colonies" in ways consistent with their religious beliefs.

In keeping with this generous policy, Delaware, New

York, New Hampshire, and Pennsylvania made conscientious objection a state constitutional right, and Madison, during the debates in the First Congress on the Bill of Rights, proposed that it be made a national constitutional right. This was to be done by including, in what became the Second Amendment, the words, "[that] no person religiously scrupulous shall be compelled to bear arms." This proposal was defeated in the Senate, probably because senators agreed with a member of the House of Representatives who said this was a matter to be left to the "benevolence of the Legislature." So it has been—subject, however, to the approval of the Supreme Court—and it is the Court's handling of the issue that justifies attention here.

No legal objections were raised when Congress (in the second of the Civil War draft acts) provided that members of religious denominations who are "conscientiously opposed to the bearing of arms, and are prohibited from doing so by the rules and articles of faith and practice of said religious denominations, shall, when drafted into the military service, be considered non-combatants, and shall be assigned by the Secretary of War to duty in the hospitals, or to the care of freedmen. . . ."

The Supreme Court first became involved in this matter during World War I when it upheld the constitutionality of the Selective Service Act of 1917 against, among others, the claim that by compelling military service, the law was a form of involuntary servitude in violation of the Thirteenth Amendment. To this, a unanimous Court said, "As we are unable to conceive upon what theory the exaction by government from the citizen of the performance of his supreme and noble duty of contributing to the defense of the rights and honor of the nation as the result of a war declared by the great representative body of the people can be read to be the

imposition of involuntary servitude, in violation of the prohibitions of the 13th Amendment, we are constrained to the
conclusion that the contention to that effect is refuted by its
mere statement." The syntax is opaque, but the sentiment is
clear enough: Citizens are supposed to be patriots.

Nothing even remotely resembling that sentiment can be
found in the Court's opinions in the years of the Vietnam
War. In 1965 and again in 1970, the Court had cases involving persons who refused to sign the statement, contained in
the Selective Service form, that they were, "by reason of
[their] religious training and belief, conscientiously opposed
to participation in war in any form." The Court nevertheless
upheld their right to exemption under the statute on the
ground that their moral views were "deeply held," and not
even the three dissenters in the 1970 case uttered a word
about a citizen's duty to serve his country.

The early history of religious exemptions suggests that
the Framers of the Constitution, and those who preceded
them in the Continental Congress, were willing to make an
exception to the general rule that everyone must obey the
law requiring military service so long as the "religiously
scrupulous" objectors were few in number. Thanks to the
Supreme Court, the exception has become the rule for anyone willing to invoke it. (Rather than complain of the Court's
misreading of the statute, Congress responded by abolishing conscription and relying on a voluntary army and navy.)

While liberalizing the statutory right of conscientious
objection, the Court has never declared it—or, for that matter, civil disobedience—a constitutional right. The general
rule continues to be that everyone is obliged to obey the law,
even if the law in question is privately thought to be a violation of the moral law. Nevertheless, when the courts handed
down decisions permitting abortion and physician-assisted

suicide, one prominent Catholic priest suggested that conscientious citizens need not obey the decisions. "Among the
most elementary principles of Western Civilization," he
writes, "is the truth that laws which violate the moral law are
null and void and must in conscience be disobeyed." He
claims this is "the principle invoked by the founders of this
nation," but he is mistaken, obviously and demonstrably
mistaken.

The Founders did not appeal to conscience, nor were they
objecting to a particular law. Their complaint was with a
"prince [who was] unfit to be the ruler of a free people," and
they claimed the right to "alter and abolish" the government
he had imposed on them. There was nothing "civil" in their
disobedience; they took up arms and made a revolution.
Were they to succeed—and, of course, they did succeed—
they would "institute new Government, laying its foundation on such principles and organizing its powers in such
form, as to them shall seem most likely to effect their Safety
and Happiness." This they did, and among the principles of
their new government is the one requiring everyone to obey
the law regardless of his religious or other private beliefs.

———•———

This is not everything that has to be said about religion under the Constitution. The point also has to be made—in
fact, it has to be emphasized—that the Founders did not attempt to discourage religious belief; on the contrary, within
the limits imposed by their Lockean principles, they intended to promote or protect it. They did so because they
had reason to believe that, in certain important respects, the
religious make better citizens than do the irreligious. This
was likely because, having been taught by Jesus to love their
neighbors as they love themselves, and by Paul (in his Epistle

to the Romans) that they are "members one of another," Christians (and most Americans were Christians) are more likely than the irreligious to come to the aid of their fellow citizens in time of need and, generally, to see themselves as members of a community to which they have obligations.

This was surely the judgment of John Witherspoon, who, by any fair reckoning, deserves to be numbered among the Founders of this country. A theologian of note in his native Scotland, Witherspoon came to America in 1768 as a professor and president of the College of New Jersey (now Princeton University). He immediately set about healing the factional divisions within his church, so that, thanks largely to his efforts, by 1780 there were some five hundred Presbyterian congregations in America, most of them in the middle and southern states (or colonies).

At the same time, he revised the College of New Jersey's curriculum with a view to preparing students for "public usefulness," and his success can be measured by the number of his students who went on to hold public office during the early years of the Republic. Among them were—I am quoting a recent Ph.D. dissertation on Witherspoon—"twelve members of the Continental Congress; five delegates to the Constitutional Convention; one U.S. president (James Madison, B.A., 1771); a U.S. vice president (Aaron Burr, B.A., 1772); forty-nine U.S. Representatives; twenty-eight U.S. Senators; three Supreme Court Justices; eight U.S. District Court Judges; one Secretary of State; three Attorneys General; and two foreign ministers," as well as numerous state judges and legislators. Quite a record for a college that had thought of itself primarily as a divinity school.

But there was nothing incongruous or inappropriate about this, not so far as Witherspoon was concerned. Benjamin Franklin might complain of a pastor's sermon because

its aim was "to make us Presbyterians [rather] than good citizens," but they were one and the same for Witherspoon, or,
as he would have said, the good Presbyterian, indeed the
good Christian, *is* the good American citizen. He was, of
course, a Scot and therefore a British subject by birth, and he
remained a Scot for the first forty-five years of his life, yet he
was the first person in New Jersey to come out in favor of
American independence. Then, as a member of the Continental Congress, he signed the Declaration of Independence (the only clergyman to do so) and played a role in the
drafting of the Articles of Confederation; and, in December
1787, he was a member of the New Jersey legislature that
ratified the Constitution.

Ever the parson as well as politician, he drafted the
proclamation issued by the Continental Congress on December 11, 1776, calling upon the various states "to implore of
Almighty God the forgiveness of the many sins prevailing
among the ranks, and to beg the countenance and assistance
of his Providence in the prosecution of the present just and
necessary war," and recommending to both civil and military officers "the exercise of repentance and reformation."
And in 1782, at his suggestion, the Congress adopted a resolution in support of Robert Aitken's translation and printing
of the Bible, the first English language Bible published in
America. The resolution read as follows: "The United States
in Congress assembled, highly approve the pious and laud-
able undertaking of Mr. Aitken, as subservient to the interest of religion . . . and being satisfied . . . of his care and
accuracy in the execution of the work, they recommend this
edition of the Bible to the inhabitants of the United States."
So far as we know, no one objected that this violated the
principle of the separation of church and state; Witherspoon was surely not of a mind to do so.

What is especially interesting about Witherspoon, and justifies the attention paid to him here, is that he was a devout Christian as well as something of a political theorist. Like Jefferson and Madison, he had obviously read Locke with care and was persuaded by him of the importance of liberty of conscience—which put him at odds with the founder of Presbyterianism, John Calvin*—and he acknowledged his debt to the Scottish Lockean, Francis Hutcheson, and to the Third Earl of Shaftesbury, who as a young man had been tutored by Locke. Thus, Witherspoon could speak unreservedly of "natural liberty" and "natural rights"; and of the "state of nature" and, like Locke (see *Treatises* II, sec. 13), of its "inconveniences," inconveniences that caused men to leave it for "the social state." But in the same lecture he could admonish his listeners and readers to accept "Christ Jesus as he is offered in the gospel," for, "except that a man be born again, he cannot see the kingdom of God." In a word, Witherspoon saw no conflict between the new political philosophy and the old religion, which is to say, between the principles set down in the Declaration of Independence and what he understood as orthodox Christianity.

In this, Witherspoon was not alone; indeed, unlike Jefferson, Madison, and others, the majority of ordinary Americans at the time were probably of the same persuasion, taking it for granted that nature's God, who endowed them with unalienable rights, including liberty of conscience, was the providential God of the Bible. However wrong as a matter of doctrine—where does the Bible speak of unalienable or natural rights, or of the liberty to worship or not to wor-

---

*For Calvin, liberty of conscience meant just that, and no more than that. If someone gave voice to his conscience, thus being heard or read by others, he might rightly be punished. So it was that, as the effective governor of his city of Geneva, Calvin had one of his anti-Trinitarian critics put to death.

ship as one pleases?—this made good political sense in America. Tocqueville recognized this in the 1830s. "Americans," he writes, "combine the notions of Christianity and of liberty so intimately in their minds that it is impossible to make them conceive the one without the other." But, if Tocqueville was right, these same Americans were of the opinion that, in politics, what mattered was not Christianity in particular but religion in general. He continues:

Religion in America takes no direct part in the government of society, but it must be regarded as the first of their political institutions; for if it does not impart a taste for freedom, it facilitates the use of it. Indeed, it is in this same point of view that the inhabitants of the United States themselves look upon religious belief. I do not know whether all Americans have a sincere faith in their religion—for who can search the human heart?—but I am certain that they hold it to be indispensable to the maintenance of republican institutions.

In the light of this assessment of American opinion, it is instructive to notice again that the Constitution leaves religion unendowed. I mean by this that, whereas (for a telling example) it grants Congress the power "to promote the Progress of Science and useful Arts" (see Article 1, section 8[8]), it nowhere gives it the power to promote religious belief. Rather, the First Amendment seems to deny it such power. But if, as Washington said in his Farewell Address, religion and morality are "indispensable," the "firmest props of the duties of Men and citizens," and if, as he also said, it is not likely that "morality can be maintained without religion," then, in the absence of federal authority, and the necessity being plain, the promotion of religious belief had to be the responsibility of the states.

In fact, it was a responsibility formally assigned to them. On July 13, 1787, even as the Constitution was being written in Philadelphia, the Continental Congress adopted an ordinance for the government of the Northwest Territory, consisting of fourteen sections and six articles, three of them germane to the subject of religion. Article 1 provided that "no person, demeaning himself in a peaceable and orderly manner, shall ever be molested on account of his mode of worship, or religious sentiments, in the said territory"; Article 3, that "religion, morality, and knowledge being necessary to good government and the happiness of mankind, schools and the means of education shall forever be encouraged"; and Article 5, that the constitutions and governments of the states to be formed out of the Northwest Territory—these proved to be Ohio, Indiana, Michigan, Illinois, and Wisconsin—"shall be republican, and in conformity to the principles contained in these articles." But the states needed no such encouragement; they took it for granted that religion was "necessary to good government," and, therefore, made it a part of the public school curriculum (see chapter 4).

———

I have made much of what the Founders hoped to accomplish by separating church and state. Unlike their counterparts in France, however, they did not intend to discourage religious belief. Rather than being content to consign religion to the private sphere, the French revolutionists abolished the Church, seized its property, and killed thousands of its priests and prelates. Then, by way of demonstrating their determination to rid themselves of every vestige of their Christian (indeed, their religious) inheritance, they replaced the Gregorian calendar with one devoid of any eccle-

siastical connections.* Our Founders, of course, did none of
these things, which goes far to explain why our revolution
concluded in the writing and ratification of a constitution
that has lasted to this day and the French in chaos and the
Terror.

Viewing it at the time from across the channel, Edmund
Burke, the Anglo-Irish statesman and political theorist,
described the French Revolution as an "extraordinary convulsion," a revolution in "sentiments, manners and moral
opinions," in other words, a complete break with the past;
but that is not what we did. Our political institutions were
refashioned in accordance with Locke's universal principles,
but (although they, too, were to change in time) our social
institutions remained much as they had been.† And prominent among them were our religious institutions. Knowing
this, the Founders did nothing to discourage religious belief;
they discouraged religious fanaticism, or, better, they hoped
to deprive it of political influence.

The Constitution, they said, was intended to provide a
"remedy for the diseases most incident to republican government," and *Federalist* 10 leaves no doubt as to what they
understood to be a disease: "tyrannical majorities," "angry

---

*The revolutionary calendar counted the years not from the birth of Jesus but
from the birth of the First Republic (in what we know as 1792), gave the months
new names (beginning with *Vendémiaire* [Vintage] and *Brumaire* [Mist], and ending with *Thermidor* [Heat] and *Fructidor* [Fruits]), prescribed that the year should
begin on September 22 (or in the new calendar, 1 *Vendémiaire*, which, that year, was
the date of the autumnal equinox) rather than on January 1, the day on which Jesus was supposed to have been circumcised, and, finally, replaced the Biblical week
of seven days with a *décade* of ten.

†In this connection, it is important to note that, unlike the French Revolution (to say nothing of the Russian), ours was not the product of a class struggle.
Tocqueville understood this very well. As he puts it, "The great advantage of the
Americans is that they have arrived at a state of democracy without having to endure a democratic revolution, and that they [were] born equal instead of becoming so."

and malignant passions," a "factious spirit," and, of most relevance here, zealous opinions "concerning religion." With these diseases in mind, they wrote a constitution that withholds, checks, and separates powers, and (see *Federalist* 63) excludes the people "*in the collective capacity*" from any share in the exercise of these powers, and consigns religion to the private sphere by separating church and state and prohibiting religious tests for officeholders. Their purpose was to exclude, or at least inhibit, the zealous, the angry, and the morally indignant, and this, in turn, depended on confining the business of government to issues less likely to give rise to zeal, anger, or moral indignation. In the private sphere, Americans would be divided by their religious beliefs, and the government would leave them alone; publicly or politically, they would be divided by their commercial interests: "a landed interest, a manufacturing interest, a mercantile interest, a moneyed interest, [and] many lesser interests," and these would have to be regulated. In fact, as Madison says (again in *Federalist* 10), "The regulation of these various and interfering interests forms the principal task of modern legislation."

America was to be a commercial republic because it promised to be both prosperous and peaceful: peaceful because prosperous, and prosperous because its people would be active and competitive. And with religion consigned to the private sphere, there would be no reason for them not to be patriots. All this the Founders learned from Locke and other modern political philosophers.

COMMERCE AND
COUNTRY

Could we convert a city into a kind of fortified camp, and infuse into each breast
so martial a genius, and such a passion for public good, as to make everyone willing to undergo the greatest hardships for the sake of the public, these affections
might now, as in ancient [Sparta and Rome], prove alone a sufficient spur to industry, and support the community. . . . But as these principles are too disinter-
ested and too difficult to support, it is requisite to govern men by other passions,
and animate them with a spirit of avarice and industry, art and luxury.

David Hume, "Of Commerce"

Happy families are all alike; every unhappy family is
unhappy in its own way." So begins Tolstoy's *Anna
Karenina*. The American story begins in 1776 when we, as
"one people," declared our independence and our right to
constitute a government, but at the same time, in the same
document, recognized each individual's right to be happy, or
unhappy, in his own way.

From this it might appear that we came together only in order to live apart, as if, having constituted the society, we were thenceforth free to think only of ourselves. A foolish opinion, no doubt, but Alexis de Tocqueville thought that democracies especially would have to contend with it and with the habits it engenders. He gave it a name: individualism. "Individualism," he writes, "disposes each member of the community to sever himself from the mass of his fellows and to draw apart with his family and his friends, so that after he has thus formed a little circle of his own, he willingly leaves society at large to itself." Leaves it to itself and leaves it to take care of itself; an individualist is the opposite of a patriot.

The Framers were not unaware of the problem. Speaking at the Constitutional Convention on June 8, 1787, James Wilson said we were "a nation of brethren," thereby minimizing what some today celebrate as our differences, and to the same end, John Jay, writing in *Federalist* 2, emphasizes, and in the process probably exaggerates, our homogeneity:

Providence has been pleased to give this one connected country to one united people—a people descended from the same ancestors, speaking the same language, professing the same religion, attached to the same principles of government, very similar in their manners and customs and who, by their joint counsels, arms, and efforts, fighting side by side throughout a long and bloody war, have nobly established their general liberty and independence.

I say probably exaggerates because Jay had to know that the Tories (not all of whom had fled the country for England or Canada) were not attached to the principles of the Revolution; "throne and altar" people, Tories paid obeisance to George III, who, as head of both state and church, ruled "by the grace of God" (*Dei Gratia, Rex*, as the motto has it) rather than with or by the consent of the people. And Jay had to know that there were people in his state of New York who were descended from ancestors different from his own, and, for another example, people in Pennsylvania for whom English was, at best, a second language; and, finally, he had to know that not all Americans professed the same religion. Yet, his exaggeration served an important political purpose: it pointed to the importance of unity and the dangers of disunity, or, to employ a term the Founders never used, of diversity.

The same concern for unity—or, as Jay put it, a similarity of manners, customs, and, above all, opinion concerning the principles of government—is reflected in the early statements and congressional debates having to do with immigration and naturalization. These debates took place in 1790 and 1794, and everyone who addressed the issue favored population growth and, to that end, a liberal immigration policy, but, at the same time, recognized the importance of excluding the immigrant who, in James Madison's words, could not readily "incorporate himself into our society," or, as Theodore Sedgwick put it, would not "mingle [here] in social affection with each other, or with us," or, finally, "would not be attached to the principles of the government of the United States." As Thomas Jefferson said, "Every species of government has its specific principles [and] ours perhaps are more peculiar than those of any other in the universe."

Jefferson, of course, knew nothing of those who would be of concern to later generations, the fascists and communists; he was concerned with monarchists and even the immigrants who had been ruled by monarchs. He was afraid that these immigrants would bring with them "the principles of the governments they leave, imbibed in their early youth; or, if able to throw them off, it [would] be in exchange for an unbounded licentiousness, passing, as is usual, from one extreme to another." Those principles, he continued, they might transmit to their children. "In proportion to their numbers, they will share with us the legislation [and] will infuse into it their spirit, warp and bias its directions, and render it a heterogeneous, incoherent, distracted mass." Immigrants were to be assimilated, incorporated into "our society," so that they, like the native born, would see this as their country, and their children would come to see it as "the mansion of their fathers," with the expectation that they would be attached to its principles and, like "the patriots of seventy-six," be prepared to defend them.

What makes us "one people" is not where we were born but, rather, our attachment to those principles of government, namely, that all men are created equal insofar as they are equally endowed by nature's God with the unalienable rights to life, liberty, and the pursuit of happiness, and that the purpose of government is "to secure these rights." This was to be done—because, according to those principles it had to be done—only with the consent of the governed. In our case, the gaining of consent to the Constitution consumed the better part of a year.

It might have taken even longer, and the government might have taken a different form, had Jefferson been on the scene (rather than in Paris) at the time the Constitution was being written and ratified. Even without him, the Anti-Federalist opposition almost prevailed and, given the weight accorded his views, probably would have prevailed had he been able to join them in the ratification debate. On the whole, he shared the views of the Anti-Federalists. Like his fellow Virginian Patrick Henry, he believed that rights were better secured at the state level; like Brutus (Robert Yates?) of New York, he believed that republican government required a similarity of "manners, sentiments, and interests"; like Mercy Warren of Massachusetts, he believed that the republican spirit was endangered by the "thirst for wealth" and the restless ambition in the heart of every man; and like Melancton Smith of New York, he thought that political power ought to be vested in the "substantial yeomanry of the country [who] are more temperate, of better morals, and less ambitious than the great." Unlike Agrippa (James Winthrop?) of Massachusetts, he did not propose a ban on foreign immigration because the states ought "to keep their blood pure"; but what he did propose for Virginia would have had the same effect. Even without a law excluding them, no foreigners would immigrate to his Virginia.

Jefferson's views on these subjects were expressed in his *Notes on the State of Virginia,* published in 1787 and the only book to come from his pen. There, but not only there, he made his case for a simple agrarian society that, because everyone would have the same interest, would be unlike the society favored in and fostered by the Constitution as we know it. There would be no assiduous merchants in his America; no bankers, active mechanics, or industrious manufacturers to compete politically with those who labor in the earth. "Our work shops [would] remain in Europe." As he attests in a famous statement, "Those who labor in the earth are the chosen people of God, if ever he had a chosen people, whose breasts he had made his peculiar deposit for substantial and genuine virtue." Republican government requires a virtuous people, and "corruption of morals in the mass of cultivators is a phaenomenon of which no age nor nation has furnished an example." Corruption, he says, will be found among those who depend on "the casualties and

caprice of customers" for their subsistence, unlike the husbandman who depends on his "own soil and industry."

But Jefferson would have been hard pressed to furnish an
example of republican government in a nation consisting
only of farmers. As one of his critics has pointed out, "A
purely agrarian society once subsisted upon the soil of western Europe, and its system was known as feudalism," and
the "mass of cultivators" were known as serfs. Knowing that
feudalism, with its "pseudo-aristocracy," depended on the
stability of land ownership, Jefferson drafted the bills abolishing primogeniture and entail in his state of Virginia.*
This, he writes, "laid the axe to the foot of the pseudo-
aristocracy"; but, by making land a commodity, to be bought
or sold as readily as a stock, bond, or bale of cotton, it also
laid the axe to his agrarian society. His bill abolishing entails
enabled "tenants in fee-tail to convey their lands in fee-
simple," and, because there was money to be made, convey
them they did, the great families and Jefferson's "husband-
men" alike.† Thanks to his "reforms," the farmer also came
to depend on the "casualties and caprice of customers."

---

*Under the law of *primogeniture* (or firstborn), title to land was given to the el-
dest son in preference to the other children; *entail* restricted the inheritance of
land to a particular class of issue.

†By way of demonstrating that property will be conveyed when it is not en-
tailed, I offer this inscription carved in stone at the gate of the most splendid estate in the nation's capital, Dumbarton Oaks:

*In 1702 The Rock of Dumbarton was granted by Queen Anne to Colonel Ninian
Beall—in 1717 Colonel George Beall, his son, added to his lands. In 1780 Thomas Beall,
his son, sold the property to William Dorsey and in 1801 William Hammond Dorsey
built this house. In 1805 he sold it to Robert Beverley who named it Acrolophos House. In
1822 he bequeathed it to James Bradshaw Beverley. James Edward Calhoun bought the
property in 1823. In 1829 Brook Mackall purchased the land and sold it in 1846 to Edward Magruder Linthicum. He enlarged the house and garden, changed the name to
Monterry and bequeathed it in 1869 to Edweard Linthicum Dent. In 1891 Henry Fitch
Blount bought the property and named it The Oaks. His widow sold it to Mildred and*

The fact is, the Federalists, and particularly James Madison and Alexander Hamilton, had a better understanding of the character of the American people, and of the form of government in which their rights could be secured. The characteristic that Tocqueville would later call their "breathless cupidity" was remarked by Hamilton even at the time of the Founding. It was he who said that all Americans—"the assiduous merchant, the laborious husbandman, the active mechanic, and the industrious manufacturer"—were looking forward "with eager expectation and growing alacrity to this pleasing reward of their toils," and this could be done "by multiplying the means of gratification [and] promoting the introduction and circulation of the precious metals, those darling objects of human avarice and enterprise" (*Federalist* 12).

Not for him was an agrarian society modeled (as Jefferson's could have been) on Jean-Jacques Rousseau's (imaginary?) country "in the vicinity of Neufchatel," a country of "happy farmers, all in comfortable circumstances, free of poll-taxes, duties, commissioners, and forced labor, cultivat[ing] with all possible care lands the produce of which is theirs, and employ[ing] the leisure that tillage leaves them to make countless artifacts with their hands and to put to use the inventive genius which nature gave them" ("Letter to M. d'Alembert on the Theatre"). Hamilton had read John Locke on property, Adam Smith's *Wealth of Nations*, and Hume's essay "On Commerce," and learned from all of them

---

Robert Wood Bliss who remodelled the house, added to the grounds, enlarged the gardens and rechristened the whole Dumbarton Oaks in 1920.

The end of the story came in 1940 when the property was conveyed to Harvard University. Families come and go, but Harvard abides, Harvard and the federal government. Incidentally, R. W. Bliss made his fortune selling a children's laxative.

that commercial republicanism promised not only prosperity but (in Smith's words) "order and good government, and, with them, the liberty and security of individuals."

Hamilton's role in the Founding is sometimes forgotten. He was largely responsible for the calling of the convention that drafted the Constitution in 1787 and for its ratification by his state of New York (by the narrow margin of 30–27) in 1788; and, as secretary of the treasury and the most influential member of President Washington's first administration, he restored the public credit by funding the national debt, established the first Bank of the United States, and wrote the great state paper, the "Report on Manufactures." As much as anyone else, and more than most, he launched the country on its way to becoming a great commercial—and unified—republic.* Still, it was Madison, taking his bearings from Hume's essays (particularly, the essays "On Commerce," "Of Parties in General," and the "Idea of a Perfect Commonwealth"), who explained the virtues of commerce in a large republic.

Madison's analysis (in *Federalist* 10) is too well known to require elaboration here. The "first object of government," he writes, is "the protection of different and unequal faculties of acquiring property," and, in an area as large as the United States, this will give rise to a variety of interests, making it "less probable that a majority of the whole will have a common motive to invade the rights of other citi-

*Despite his considerable achievements, Hamilton is not much honored today, not even in the nation's capital. The name of his great adversary, Thomas Jefferson, is attached not only to a memorial but to a street, a place, and (adjoining and running parallel to the Mall) a drive, as well as to a hotel, a "corner," an institute for justice, a condominium, and a host of other private institutions; but, aside from the statue of him outside the Treasury Building, Hamilton rates only one lonely street (on the "wrong" side of the city), an insurance company, and (perhaps significantly) an income tax service. It is as if he was only a minor figure in this country's early history, rather like Roger Sherman or Daniel of St. Thomas Jenifer.

zens." It will not be a society of Good Samaritans; it will, however, be a society whose members are not so likely to fall among thieves when traveling the road from Jerusalem to Jericho (or Boston to New York), because the passions of men will be directed into activities that do not lead to bloodshed and do not threaten the peace. As Montesquieu says in his famous *Spirit of the Laws* (and both Madison and Hamilton refer to him as "the celebrated Montesquieu"), "Commerce cures destructive prejudices; and it is almost a general rule that wherever there are soft morals, there is commerce; and wherever there is commerce, there are soft morals." And chief among the "destructive prejudices" to be cured by commerce is the Christian doctrine that acquisitiveness—or greed, to give it the ugly name it used to bear, or covetousness—is one of the seven mortal sins. When no longer seen as a sin, acquisitiveness can be the means of promoting the public good, or, to say the same thing, of solving the political problem.

So said Madison, and his solution can be expressed in a formula: a competition of economic interests rather than an animosity of religious factions. This economic competition will be peaceful because, when properly regulated—and the regulation of "these various and interfering interests forms the principal task of modern legislation"—everyone (or, as Locke would have it, everyone except the idle and quarrelsome) will prosper to a greater or lesser extent and, as a result, everyone will recognize a common interest in preserving a government that secures everyone's rights to life, liberty, and the pursuit of a self-defined happiness. This society will have less need of Samaritans, but, as Locke and his followers would have said, there were never many Good Samaritans anyway.

But Rousseau, the most thoughtful of Locke's critics, had

already—that is, even before our founding—cast doubt on the viability of a Lockean commercial republic. In the first place, Rousseau argued that one of the most important tasks of government was to prevent "extreme inequality of wealth, not by taking treasures away from those who possess them, but by removing the means of accumulating them from everyone; not by building poor houses, but by protecting citizens from becoming poor." If there are no limits on acquisition, he suggested, wealth would be concentrated in the hands of a few, and the poor would be dispossessed even of the huts they built with their own hands. "Aren't all the advantages of society for the powerful and the rich? Aren't all the lucrative jobs filled by them alone? Aren't all the pardons and all the exemptions reserved for them? And isn't public authority entirely in their favor? . . . How different is the picture of the poor man! The more humanity owes him, the more society refuses him." Rousseau was not a communist, but on this subject he anticipated Karl Marx by a hundred years. As we now know, however, Rousseau and Marx were wrong, and Locke was right; despite inequalities of wealth, the working man has not been impoverished in the commercial society. But more to the point, Rousseau doubted that self-interested men could be made into patriotic citizens, and by self-interested men he meant what Locke and the Declaration of Independence meant, namely, men endowed by nature's God with the private rights to life, liberty, and the pursuit of happiness, but whose only duties are of their own creation. Why should such a man, a man who institutes government in order to secure his private rights, have any concern for anyone else? Why should he be public-spirited?

Locke's answer was that he will quickly see that the rights that are his by nature cannot be secured in nature (or in the state of nature), and, being reasonable, he will see that they can be secured only under government and that it is to his advantage to obey the laws imposed on him by that government. As Locke said, he can expect to profit under a government that secures his rights and can be expected willingly to accept the duties it imposes. After all, those duties are, or will be, of his own making. But Rousseau claimed it would not work out this way. The reasonable but wicked man will understand that it is to his advantage to disobey the law when everyone else obeys it. "He is delighted that everyone, except himself, be just." Rousseau's larger point is that reasoning based on self-interest cannot lead to a concern for the well-being of others. As he puts it, "The human Race would have perished long ago if its preservation had depended only on the reasoning of its members."

There is nothing in the record to lead one to believe that Jefferson or any of the Anti-Federalists had read Rousseau; for example, his term for the sort of man who would inhabit—indeed, would come to characterize—the Lockean commercial republic does not appear in any of their writings. They did, however, seem to share his disdain, if not his contempt, for the "bourgeois," Rousseau's term for Locke's rational, industrious, and acquisitive man. Such a man, they thought, was not likely to be a good citizen. In his stead, Jefferson (as I said above) proposed the "husbandman," and the Anti-Federalists, the "substantial yeoman of sense and discernment."*

*This issue of who makes the good republican citizen surfaced during the ratification debates when the Anti-Federalists, led in New York by Melancton Smith, complained of the small size of the House of Representatives (only sixty-five members originally). Like Rousseau, Smith favored a small state and something on the order of a direct democracy, in which the people know, and resemble, one another; but, given the size of the United States, he had to settle for its closest approximation, a large number of representatives. A representative body, he writes,

Nevertheless, however much they talked of sturdy yeomen and republican virtues and small communities of brothers, in the end they too took their stand with Lockean acquisition. And so, too, did their lineal descendants of the next generation, the Jacksonians. The Jacksonians may have wanted "to preserve the virtues of a simple agrarian republic"—Marvin Meyers shows this most perceptively in his book *The Jacksonian Persuasion*—but they proved unwilling to pay the price for it. John Adams taunted the Anti-Federalists with this unwillingness. You want rustic simplicity? he asked. You want the small agrarian republic? If so, what you want is San Marino:

A handful of poor people, living in the simplest manner, by hard labor upon the produce of a few cows, sheep, goats, swine, poultry, and pigeons, on a piece of rocky snowy ground, protected from every enemy by their situation, their superstition, and even by their poverty, having no commerce or luxury. . . .

As it turned out, no one wanted San Marino or anything resembling it. Most Americans wanted what Madison, Hamilton, and the other Framers of the Constitution promised.

We might argue about whether the bourgeois is a better citizen than Jefferson's husbandman or Melancton Smith's sturdy yeoman. But there can be little doubt that the average American is better off today and, in one sense at least, freer than he was in 1787. The same can be said of the onetime slaves. They were the "mass of cultivators" in Virginia's agrarian system, and, like the serfs under feudalism, it was

---

"should be a true picture of the people," large enough to include the "substantial yeomanry of the country [who] are more temperate, of better morals and less ambitious than the great." They, not the "great" and "ambitious," make the good citizens.

their labor that made possible whatever virtue there was among the "pseudo-aristocratic" planters.

The fact is that Jefferson could no more have lived in a simple agrarian republic than Rousseau could have lived in that country "in the vicinity of Neufchatel." Rousseau was a novelist, playwright, and composer, but most of all a philosopher who numbered among his acquaintances the philosophers Voltaire, d'Alembert, Diderot, and Hume, none of whom could have been bred in a San Marino. Jefferson disliked "the mobs of the great cities," but he loved and flourished in Paris. When president, he made a point of receiving the British ambassador in homespun and carpet slippers (and was mistaken for one of the servants), but there was no mistaking his status when back home at Monticello. There, surrounded by hundreds of slaves, he dressed like the aristocrats with whom he had associated in prerevolutionary Paris. Yet, as it happened, it was from Paris that he wrote (in a letter to John Jay) that cultivators of the earth are the most valuable, the most vigorous, the most independent, the most virtuous citizens because they are "tied to their country & wedded to its liberty and interests by the most lasting bonds."

This is a venerable opinion, this association of land, or the earth, with patriotic sentiments. It is not for nothing that Shakespeare has John of Gaunt in *Richard II* end his great patriotic speech by invoking "this blessed plot, this earth, this realm, this England" (act 2, sc. 1). Even Locke, the progenitor of capitalism, in the course of explaining the origins of private property, speaks of mixing one's labor with the land. Land, a bit of land of one's own, is the most tangible (touchable), the most concrete manifestation of one's country. It cannot be moved; it is part of one's country in a way that capital investments are not. Unlike a stock portfolio, land is fixed in place, and this, as Adam Smith pointed out, has political significance. "The proprietor of land is necessarily a citizen of the particular country in which his estate lies," he writes in *The Wealth of Nations*, whereas "the proprietor of stock is properly a citizen of the world, and is not necessarily attached to any particular country." Smith was content to characterize him, but Rousseau gave him a name, the "bourgeois," and, in due course, "bourgeois bashing" became something of a way of life among intellectuals; and artists especially measure or define themselves against the bourgeois. Marx's name for him was "capitalist."

Rather than being attached to his country, the capitalist is said to be at home in the market, and the market, as we have ever greater reason to know, has no national boundaries. Not love of country, but the market determines where the capitalist buys his supplies, sells his products, and, of greatest consequence, invests his money; it also determines whom, and how many, he would allow to enter the country as immigrants. The market has its laws, or rules, but those rules are written, or discovered, by economists, not political theorists: *political* economists in Smith's day and simply economists in ours. It is an exaggeration to say that capitalists are interested only in money, but it is not much of an exaggeration to say that, since Smith, economics has taken the place of political theory, and that wealth, not justice, is what economists talk about. Rousseau was the first to note this fact. As he puts it, "Ancient political writers spoke constantly about morals and virtue; ours speak only about commerce and money."

So far as I know, Marx was the first to call America a "bourgeois society." He would not have said this of the small, essentially agrarian societies favored by the Anti-Federalists, as well as by Jefferson. But, when not used disparagingly, it is an appropriate term for what we are and were intended to be. Thomas Paine—Tom Paine as he is better known in America—might have used it in his *Common Sense*, the little book (actually a pamphlet) that sold over a hundred thousand copies in 1776 and is said to have galvanized the colonials and, beyond anything else said or written, inspired the Revolution. As he writes, "Commerce diminishes the spirit both of patriotism and military defense"; but this did not much bother him because America did not intend to set "the world at defiance." "Our plan is commerce, and that, well attended to, will secure us the peace and friendship of all Europe; because it is the interest of all Europe to have America a *free port*. [Our] trade will always be a protection, and [our] barrenness of gold and silver secure her from invaders."

In saying this, Paine was expressing the view, widely held among the philosophers of commercialism, that commerce, by softening men's morals and tastes—for example, by causing them to seek comfort rather than glory or empire, to be compassionate rather than vengeful, to go to court when insulted rather than fight a duel, to avoid being "judgmental," and so on—would render them peaceful. But Hamilton, for one, was not persuaded of this. The genius of republics is supposed to be pacific, he writes in *Federalist* 6, and the spirit of commerce is supposed to have a tendency "to soften the manners of men, and to extinguish those inflammable humors which have so often kindled into wars"; and it is said that commercial republics "will never be disposed to waste themselves in ruinous contentions with each other, [that] they will be governed by mutual interests, and will cultivate a spirit of mutual amity and concord." He thought this "visionary," belied by the examples of earlier commercial republics: Carthage, Venice, and the provinces of Holland, which "took a leading and conspicuous part in the wars of Europe."

There was, however, some truth in what Paine and the other "visionary" politicians said: there has never been a war between America and another liberal democracy. Yet, Hamilton was surely justified in predicting, or expecting, that America would be involved in wars of some sort and, therefore, that it would need an army and navy. Because he thought that the citizens of this republic would be absorbed in their private commercial pursuits and, therefore, would not take to soldiering, he suggests, in *Federalist* 8, that it would have to be defended by a standing army "distinct from the body of citizens."* But his opponents, the Anti-Federalists, doubted that a people not prepared to fight for their country would deserve to be called citizens. "What need has a virtuous people for a standing army?" they asked. In the clause providing for it (Article 1, section 8[12]), they saw evidence of the Federalists' seeming lack of concern for moral character, or for the kind of citizen required by republican government.

Admittedly, moral character did not figure much in the Founder's deliberations. Madison spoke of the need for virtue, but he seemed to take it for granted; he certainly said nothing about the need to cultivate it. Nor does the Constitution make any provision for it. In fact, the word "education" appears not at all in the Constitution, and only once in the *Federalist*, then only in passing (see *Federalist* 62).

Not surprisingly, given their concern for a "virtuous people," education, particularly religious education, was a major concern of the Anti-Federalists. For example, Charles Turner of Massachusetts said that "without the prevalence of *Christian piety and morals*, the best republican constitutions can never save us from slavery and ruin." He followed

---

*In the event, Americans—North and South—proved capable of fighting their own battles but disagreed on what they were fighting for. See chapter 5.

this by expressing the hope that the states would institute such means of education "as shall seem *adequate* to the *divine, patriotick purpose of* training up the children and youth at large, in that solid learning, and in those pious and moral principles, which are the *support,* the life and SOUL of republican government and liberty, of which a free Constitution in the body."

As I point out in the following chapter, Jefferson agreed on the need for moral or civic education, that it was the job of the states to provide it, and differed only on whether religious training should be a part of it.

EDUCATING YOUNG
PATRIOTS

It cannot be doubted that in the United States the instruction of the people pow-
erfully contributes to the support of the democratic republic; and that will always
be the case, I think, where the instruction that enlightens the mind is not sepa-
rated from the education responsible for moral-manners [*les moeurs*].

Tocqueville, *Democracy in America*

Thomas Jefferson was, as he claimed to be, "Father of the
University of Virginia," and in that capacity he proposed the teaching of John Locke's treatises and Algernon
Sidney's discourses on government, as well as other works
expounding "the general principles of liberty and the rights
of man, in nature and in society." His purpose, of course, was
to secure republican government in America by ensuring
that students be thoroughly schooled in its first principles.
But he had to know that a grasp of these principles does not
entail or necessarily promote a love of country, even of a

country deliberately founded on those principles. After all, Karl Marx—who, to say the least, was no friend of republican government—probably had a better understanding of Locke's treatises and Sidney's discourses than did any of the professors employed to teach them in Virginia.

Inculcation of a love of country, like moral education generally, takes place at an earlier age, which is why Jefferson also proposed that the young—boys and girls alike, and without regard to "wealth, birth, or other accidental condition or circumstance"—be educated at public expense. A liberal education in "reading, writing, and common arithmatick," he writes, followed by the reading of "Graecian, Roman, English, and American history," would render them "worthy to receive, and able to guard the sacred deposit of the rights and liberties of their fellow citizens."

He further proposed that these elementary schools be established and controlled locally. Let every (Virginia) county be divided into "hundreds" (or, as he later put it, "wards"), explain to the people therein the purpose of the schools, have them build "a log school-house," and defray the costs of instruction. Better, he says, that this be done by "the parents within each ward" than by the county or state (to say nothing of the national government). "Where every man is a sharer in the direction of his ward-republic . . . and feels that he is a participator in the government of affairs, not merely at an election one day in the year, but every day; when there shall not be a man in the State who will not be a member of some one of its councils, great or small, he will let the heart be torn out of his body sooner than his power be wrested from him by a Caesar or a Bonaparte." In a word, they would be patriots.

Jefferson's point was that by giving parents the ultimate responsibility for the civic education of their children, they will themselves be made better citizens, and republican government will be the beneficiary. Politically he was for states rights and, where appropriate, local power. To make this as plain as possible, he employed a classical apothegm: "As Cato concluded every speech with the words, '*Carthago delenda est*' [Carthage must be destroyed], so do I [conclude] every opinion with the injunction, 'divide the counties into wards.' Begin them only for a single purpose [of educating the young]; they will soon show for what others they are the best instruments." In short, political participation, especially at the local level, contributes to an education in republicanism. As for the importance of this, we have the word of the political philosopher Montesquieu: "It is in a republican government that the whole power of education is required."

Well before Jefferson turned to this subject, Noah Webster had published essays calling for the political education of children. "Every child in America," he writes, "should be acquainted with his own country," not only with its settlement and geography, but also with its principles and the "illustrious heroes and statesmen" responsible for its liberty. "These are interesting objects to every man," he goes on; "they call home the minds of youth and fix them upon the interests of their own country, and they assist in forming attachments to it, as well as enlarging the understanding." He devoted his life to making this possible.

In addition to being the editor of our first dictionary, Webster was an essayist, teacher, educator—in a way, our first professional educator—and the author of spellers, grammars, and other books for the young, including, in 1785, a book of readings, renamed in 1787, even as the Constitution was being written, *An American Selection of Lessons in Reading and Speaking*. This reader went through seventy-seven editions in the half-century following its first publication, educating, or helping to educate, several generations of young Americans. One can get a sense of the influence Webster intended it to have on those students from the epigraph he put on its title page, a quote from the pen of the French republican revolutionist Count Mirabeau: "Begin with the infant in the cradle; let the first word he lisps be Washington."

Webster's reader is essentially a collection of edifying stories and speeches (with instructions for reading aloud); stories about the Revolutionary War; famous American orations and state papers, including the Declaration of Independence and George Washington's farewell orders to the army; as well as extracts from the works of certain famous authors—Swift, Pope, Johnson, Shakespeare (Shakespeare's made more edifying for young Americans by careful editing), and, of particular interest, long extracts from Joseph Addison's play *Cato*.

Written in 1713 and set in the waning days of the Roman republic, the play tells the story of the legendary patriot Cato the Younger, who has withdrawn to Utica, a city on the north coast of Africa, in order to rally what is left of Rome's republican senate against the encroaching power of Julius Caesar. Although written by an Englishman, *Cato* was a favorite during the colonial period, and it became still more popular with the approach of the war with England, Caesar reminding Americans of George III, or vice versa. Its central theme is honor, which may explain its appeal for Washington. Not only did he see it performed more than once and, like those legendary American patriots Patrick Henry and Nathan Hale, quote lines from it on appropriate occasions, but, to rally their spirits, he encouraged his troops to stage a performance of it at Valley Forge during the miserable winter of 1777–78.*

*On this, and on the general subject of the political education of the young, see Lorraine Smith Pangle and Thomas L. Pangle, *The Learning of Liberty: The Educational Ideas of the American Founders* (Lawrence: University of Kansas Press, 1993).

No modern American general, not even Douglas Mac-Arthur, would hazard its performance, or anything like it, for his troops. Nor would any modern educator include it in a book of readings. Its language is too stilted for today's sophisticated students, and its moralizing too overt, but generations of this country's schoolchildren used to read *Cato* in the early nineteenth century. So, too, were succeeding generations taught to read, write, and speak, and in the process taught to love their country, from McGuffey's *Readers*, with their stories of Washington and other American heroes (killing two birds with one stone, so to speak).

Like John Witherspoon, William H. McGuffey was a Presbyterian clergyman and, from 1845 until his death in 1873, a professor, in his case, of moral philosophy at the University of Virginia. Again like Witherspoon, he took it for granted that the religious make good citizens, and, therefore, that the public schools might rightly employ religion in their educational programs.

His *Eclectic Readers* proved to be both the most popular and, in the public schools, the most widely used of schoolbooks. Originally published in four volumes, with the third and last edition coming in 1879, they were to sell more than 120 million copies in the years 1836 through 1920. The principal historian of American education estimates that half the schoolchildren of America "drew their inspiration and formulated their codes of morals and conduct from this remarkable series of Readers." But there is a marked difference between the first and last editions, a difference that has to do with religion.

In the first edition, young children were enjoined to "pray to God to keep [them] from sin and harm," and to "ask God to fill [their] hearts with love for him," and to obey his commandments because "you cannot steal the smallest pin without being seen by that eye which never sleeps"; and in a lesson entitled "More About the Bible," they were told that "the *Design of the Bible* is evidently to give us correct information concerning the creation of all things, by the omnipotent word of God; to make known to us the state of holiness and happiness of our first parents in paradise, and their dreadful fall from that condition by transgression against God, which is the original cause of all our sin and misery." The sinful were told they would go to hell (and they were left in no doubt of its existence); and that the righteous would see God "seated upon that majestic throne; and Angels in numbers more than can be counted, will fill the universe with their glittering wings and their rapturous songs." Many of the readings were taken directly from the Old and New Testaments, and the children were asked to read them aloud, and told how to read them. ("Hold your book up well and do not bend forward. Speak each word distinctly and be careful to pronounce correctly. Endeavor to understand what you read.") And all this, mind you, to the end of preparing the young to be good citizens.

In the 1879 edition, published after McGuffey's death, the Bible makes only an occasional appearance, sin almost never, and nothing is said of piety and salvation. Children are told not to covet their neighbors' riches, not because of God's commandment forbidding it, but because "God makes everybody rich." Still present are the edifying tales ("Perseverance," "Dare to Do Right," "Waste Not, Want Not," "Beware of the First Drink,") and, here and there, the admonition to pray before going to sleep. But mostly children are enjoined to be industrious, loyal to their employers, as well as frugal, reliable, and truthful.

A pious Christian, McGuffey would have deplored this shift from religious to merely moral instruction, but, given the changes in the demographic character of the population and the spread of Madisonian-Jeffersonian principles, a "watering down" of the public school curriculum was both inevitable and required.* How could the states promote religious belief if, as Madison anticipated and as in fact was increasingly the case as the nineteenth century proceeded, they had to deal with a plurality of sects, and not all of them Christian? To be specific, how could Charles Turner expect his state of Massachusetts to provide religious instruction in its schools if its residents disagreed on the tenets of religion?

Although this is not the place to recount it, the history of American elementary education is, in one significant respect, a history of the gradual secularization of the public schools and their curricula. During the colonial period and continuing into the nineteenth century, to the extent that it existed at all outside the family (or the wealthy families employing tutors for the purpose), education was the direct responsibility of the various churches. The states assumed it when they established the public schools, but, except that it ceased to be sectarian, the education they provided continued to be religious in character, consisting, as one historian says, "largely in the Bible and moralizing based on the Bible."

---

*In 1785 Madison succeeded in defeating a proposal—even though it had the support of Patrick Henry and John Marshall, the future chief justice, and initially of George Washington—that the Virginia legislature allocate funds in support of "Teachers of the Christian Religion." Not only was the bill defeated, but in 1786 the legislature adopted, instead, Jefferson's Statute for Religious Freedom.

It was on this occasion that Madison composed his famous *Memorial and Remonstrance,* addressed to the Virginia General Assembly, but, because his words carried weight, destined to affect opinion elsewhere, even to the present day. His premise was that liberty of conscience is a god-given right, and from this Madison drew the conclusion that any public program in support of religion—support of any kind, and whether of a particular religion or religion in general—was illegitimate.

The Massachusetts schools, for example, provided such education until 1827, when the state prohibited the purchase of books calculated to favor a particular sect or tenet; but the purpose of this law was merely to put an end to the monopoly then enjoyed by the Congregational Church, not to make the schools secular. Even Horace Mann, whose contribution to the cause of public education is commemorated in many a school building bearing his name, was not opposed to religion in the schools, only to sectarian schools. He was, he writes, "in favor of religious instruction in our schools to the extremest verge to which it can be carried [but] without invading those rights of conscience which are established by the laws of God and guaranteed by the Constitution of the State [of Massachusetts]."

Even though Roman Catholics were to attend their own private schools, this proved to be a difficult condition for the public schools to meet; as with school prayers, it is only a vacuous program of religious instruction that does not offend somebody's conscience. Better, then, to confine the instruction to moral lessons of the sort found in the third edition of McGuffey's *Readers*. On the other hand, one might well wonder whether his moralizing tales, or "Lessons," had the effect intended, even then. For a case in point, consider the lesson entitled "The Young Witness," a dialogue between a trial judge and a young girl appearing as a witness for the first time. Its obvious purpose was to persuade schoolchildren to tell the truth, but the young girl needed no instruction on this score; she had received all the instruction she needed from her parents. Thus, asked by the judge what would "befall" her if she did not testify truthfully, she replied, "I shall never go to heaven." Asked how she knew this, "the child took the Bible, turned rapidly to the chapter containing the commandments, and, pointing to the one which reads, 'Thou shalt not bear false witness against thy neighbor,' said, 'I learned that before I could read.'"

The force of McGuffey's lesson obviously depended on whether the Bible's precepts were, at the time (the 1870s and '80s), generally accepted as God's law and were to be obeyed in hope of salvation and fear of divine punishment. Did most Americans believe this? (Did Mark Twain's Tom Sawyer—who made his first appearance at this time—believe it?) Or had they come to believe with some prominent theologians who, even then, argued that the "truth and reality" of the Bible's laws and teaching evolve "in the process of history"? If so, and if the Bible's teachings could be dispensed with whenever they proved inconvenient—Tom Sawyer was good at this—McGuffey's moral sermons would have fallen on deaf ears. (This was probably not the case with another of his truth-telling lessons, this one featuring Parson Weems's story about George Washington and the cherry tree. The story was, of course, untrue, but the children had no reason to know this; they did, however, know that Washington was a hero and someone to emulate.)

Still, from today's perspective, it is surprising that religion continued to be a part of the public school curriculum for so long a time, specifically, for most of the nineteenth century and, in some places, continuing into the twentieth. On the other hand, there was no reason then for Americans not to agree with the Founders, many of whom had taken it for granted that belief in God and attachment to country go together, and that to promote the one is to promote the other. To repeat what Tocqueville said on this score, "Americans combine the notions of Christianity and of liberty so intimately in their minds that it is impossible to make them conceive the one without the other."

Besides, apart from the overarching principles of the Constitution, the daily life of Americans at the time—their business affairs and their relations with one other—was governed mostly by the common (or customary) law, and this law was essentially a civil version of God's commandments. Thus, it was an offense under the common law, as well as against God, to murder, commit adultery, steal, bear false witness, and fail to honor your father and mother.*

As for the Constitution, none of its principles prohibited the states from enforcing these common law provisions; more to the point, nothing in the First Amendment was then understood to prohibit the states from providing religious instruction in their schools or, in one way or another, from recognizing the connection between religious belief and republican government. It is only in our own time—or, at least, in *my* own time—that the states have ceased to do this. In fact, however, they had no choice in the matter; in a pair of decisions handed down in the 1940s, the Supreme Court held that the First Amendment prohibited the states from making any law "respecting the establishment of religion." This was a momentous decision; it was also unauthorized.

Previously, everyone having anything to do with the subject understood that the prohibitions of the First Amendment did not apply to the states, and that to change this would require a constitutional amendment. This was Madison's view. During the debates in the First Congress on the

---

*Under the common law, parents were required to care for their children, children for their parents, grandparents for their grandchildren, and grandchildren for their grandparents. The principle of *negotiorum gestio* (doing the business of another voluntarily and without authority) also made it an offense to fail to come to the aid of a neighbor; but, because of the difficulty of distinguishing between, say, a Good Samaritan and an "officious interloper," this soon fell into desuetude.

amendments that became the Bill of Rights, he proposed an additional amendment—he thought it the "most valuable amendment" in the list—forbidding the states to "violate the equal rights of conscience." After being adopted in the House of Representatives (where Madison served), the proposal went down to defeat in the Senate. Then, in 1876 Senator James G. Blaine of Maine, at the behest of President Ulysses S. Grant, proposed a somewhat similar amendment. This, too, passed in the House and went down to defeat in the Senate, coming one vote short of the required two-thirds majority. But what Madison could not do in 1789, or Grant and Blaine in 1876, a divided Supreme Court, without so much as a by-your-leave, effectively did in the 1940s.

The first of the 1940s cases involved a New Jersey statute that, leaving aside the complications, allowed parents to be reimbursed for the cost of transporting their children to school, parochial as well as public; the second, coming from Illinois, involved a "released-time" program in which public school students, with the consent of their parents, received religious instruction during school hours, in the school building, but from unpaid religious teachers (Protestant, Catholic, or Jewish).*

What is of interest in these cases, aside from the judgments rendered and the specious arguments used to support them, is the heedless manner in which they were decided. Not one of the Supreme Court justices gave any thought,

*_Everson_ v. _Board of Education_, 330 U.S. 1 (1947); _McCollum_ v. _Board of Education_, 333 U.S. 203 (1948). It was in the first of these cases that Justice Wiley B. Rutledge said that the purpose of the First Amendment "was to create a complete and permanent separation of the spheres of religious activity and civil authority by comprehensively forbidding every form of public aid or support for religion." Unless he intended deliberately to deceive, no one with any knowledge of our history could have written this.

any thought whatsoever, to the role of religion in republican government, specifically, the connection, or even the possibility of a connection, between religious training and the sort of citizen required by a self-governing republic. They simply did not address the issue, as if the cases being decided had nothing to do with it, or as if it were of no importance; nor did they attempt to refute or question it. As a consequence, moral education, which had always been understood to be partly a public responsibility, was now held to be exclusively a private one, to be performed, in part, by the churches, but mostly by the parents in the home. Presumably, they will want to teach their children "values," as we now say, but, if so, they will get little help from the law.*

The purpose of those school laws was to endow children with a love of country, and to transmit this from one generation to the next. The question now is whether this can be done by parents on their own, or with the help of the secularized public schools. As stated, this is a new question, but the underlying issue is as old as the Constitution; it has to do with the moral character of the American people. On this, Madison, for one, seems to have been confident. Contrary to some critics of the Constitution who doubted it, he says there was "sufficient virtue among [us] for self-government" (see *Federalist* 55). By virtue he meant one of those "qualities" the possession of which leads a naturally self-interested or selfish person to be public-spirited. In this sense, virtue is, or requires, self-restraint, which, it is important to note, is not how it had been understood previously.

---

*They will get no help whatsoever from the law when—or if—they attempt to impose some restrictions on what their children read, see, or otherwise enjoy. The Supreme Court put the censors out to pasture some thirty years ago, and did so with the assurance that it doesn't really matter what children read, see, or enjoy. As one justice said, and he was speaking for the majority of the Court, "One man's vulgarity is another's lyric" (*Cohen* v. *California*, 403 U.S. 15, 25 [1971]).

Previously, virtue had little to do with self-restraint. The word itself derives from the Latin *vir*, meaning man, and *virtus*, meaning manliness; hence, the four classical (or "cardinal") virtues: prudence, temperance, fortitude, and justice. These are qualities intended to define a man, and, without going into the complications, the men possessing them were thought to be entitled to rule. In short, they are the virtues appropriate to an aristocracy.*

It was not Madison, but the man he called "the celebrated Montesquieu," who first redefined virtue, making it appropriate to a regime founded on the new republican or democratic principles; as Montesquieu says, the situation required him "to find new words or to give to old words new meanings." And he does the latter with virtue. Under its new meaning, it is "neither a moral virtue nor a Christian virtue [i.e., faith, hope, and love of God]; it is a *political* virtue," a virtue manifested in a self-sacrificing love of country. Love of country, or patriotism, is possible under any form of government, but it is particularly "felt" in a democracy because only there is it possible for citizens to identify themselves with the whole community. But to say it is "felt," rather than comprehended, means that it is a passion, or, as he says, a "sensation," and not a product of the understanding. This is important because a sensation "may be felt by the meanest as well as by the highest person in the state." If so, and Madison said it was so at our beginning, the question is whether it will remain so over time.

---

*Not surprisingly, Winston Churchill—an anachronism even in his own day—understood the term in this old-fashioned way. According to one of his biographers, he once offered a cigar to John Rotherstein, the director of London's Tate Gallery, who refused it, saying, "Every man should have one virtue." (His was not smoking.) Churchill replied, "There is no such thing as a negative virtue. If I have been of any service to my fellow men, it has never been by self-repression, but always by self-expression."

Montesquieu (at first glance) seems to have been hopeful about this. Virtue in a republic is a "very simple" thing, he says. It is love of country, "and to inspire it ought to be the principal business of education: but the surest way of instilling it into children is for parents to set them an example." Which is to say, if parents make a point of loving their country, their children will also come to love it—unless, he adds, "impressions made at home are effaced by those they have received abroad." Virtue may be a "very simple thing," but transmitting it from one generation to the next is not a simple matter; it depends on families that are impervious to, or able to protect their children from, the baneful impressions likely to be received from abroad (*du dehors*, in the French), by which he means the world outside the family.*

Whatever "abroad" meant for Montesquieu in the mid–eighteenth century, for us today it means, among other things, the films the young see, the television they watch—according to a recent poll, 53 percent of them have television sets in their bedrooms—the music they hear, and the Internet they "surf." Montesquieu obviously knew nothing about these products of modern science, but he had reason to know that, once available, there would be men willing to exploit them for profit and without regard to their effect on the young. Nor did he expect many parents to object. As he writes, "It is not young people who degenerate; they are ruined only when grown men have already been corrupted." Carried forward, this means that, when grown, today's young will corrupt tomorrow's, even as they were corrupted by yes-

---

*Tocqueville provides the best explanation of why the aristocratic family was not faced with this problem; it was a world unto itself. "Among aristocratic nations," he says, "as families remain for centuries in the same condition, often on the same spot, all generations become, as it were, contemporaneous. A man almost always knows his forefathers and respects them; he thinks he already sees his remote descendants and he loves them" (*Democracy in America*, vol. 2, book 2, chap. 2).

terday's. And where, in this chain of generations, will virtue be found?

Montesquieu discusses these matters in book 4 (see especially chapter 5) of his *Spirit of the Laws,* and, according to one authority, "his point seems to be that those regimes that depend for their existence on the inculcation and transmission of virtue through the generations are doomed to decline." We would like to reject his conclusion, but not many of us would deny his premise that the health of a republic depends on the moral health of its citizens. Kings might rule without it, and despots have reason to fear it, but republics depend on virtue as Montesquieu defines it.

As I indicated earlier, Madison took this for granted, and, with this in mind, he said there was "sufficient virtue" among the American people. Jefferson agreed, but he wondered—in fact, he very much doubted—whether this would be true in the days to come. "Our rulers will become corrupt," he predicted in 1781, "our people careless," so careless as to forget what was expected of them. "They will forget themselves, but in the sole faculty of making money." For these and other reasons, he thought our prospects grim: "From the conclusion of this war we shall be going down hill."

He apparently believed that war brings out the best in a people, but, as he said a few years later, "war is not the best engine for us to resort to." Other "engines" had to be found, other ways of securing a happy future, other means of fostering those habits and actions that he held to be the foundation of republican government. Out of his preoccupation with this problem came a host of proposals, including those having to do with education: the schools, at every level, were to play an important role in the fostering of those virtuous habits and transmitting them from one generation to the next. But the schools today are a far cry from what Jefferson expected and would have required them to be.

Not only did he expect schools to provide instruction in Greek, Latin, geography, and the higher branches of numerical arithmetic, and Grecian, Roman, and American history, but, without employing religion for the purpose, he expected them to instill "the first elements of morality" into children's minds. Like Webster and McGuffey, he believed it essential that children be taught to love their country, and he further believed this country especially deserved to be loved, because it was good or just. This assumes—and in 1776 we held it to be a fact—that there are standards by which countries are to be judged, but this is denied today. Thus, for one example, in 1991 the state of Florida enacted a statute requiring its public schools to teach that no "culture is intrinsically superior or inferior to another," which is a way of saying to its most recent immigrants that they might just as well have stayed in Cuba or Haiti, as if there is nothing to choose between Castro's dictatorship and constitutional democracy, or Haitian voodooism and the biblical religions. Any standard by which "cultures" might be judged will be said to be a product of a particular culture—that is, our culture—and has no relevance elsewhere.

If taken seriously, cultural or moral relativism makes it difficult, if not impossible, for the schools to do what they have traditionally been expected to do, namely, to play a major role in the making of public-spirited citizens. How can the schools teach students to love their country and be prepared to make sacrifices for it, when telling them that its "culture" or form of government is no better than any other country's? The Founders could speak of "civilized nations," as opposed to "savage tribes" and "barbarians," and did so because they thought the distinction important (see *Federalist* 10, 24, 41). But no such distinction can be made today; teachers may speak of cultural differences, but they may not make any distinction implying a judgment. In this new moral order, tolerance, blind tolerance, is the virtue taught, and "judgmentalism" is the vice.

This was not the case in 1776, when, among other things, we accused our "British brethren" of being "deaf to the voice of justice." Nor was it the case in the mid–nineteenth century when the issue of slavery threatened a permanent rift in the nation. We fought a war to prevent that, and Lincoln, who was the best of us, used that war to bring out the best in the rest of us. How he did this is the subject of the next chapter.

LINCOLN,
PATRIOTISM'S POET

I do not wish to speak ill of war; war almost always widens a nation's mental
horizons and raises its heart. In some cases it may be the only factor which can
prevent the exaggerated growth of certain inclinations naturally produced by
equality and be the antidote needed for certain inveterate diseases to which
democratic societies are liable.

Tocqueville, *Democracy in America*

When Alexander Hamilton said that American habits
were incompatible with soldiering, he overlooked
the fact that we had only recently fought and won the Revolutionary War, and that he, commander of the New York
company of light infantry that played a decisive role in the
final battle at Yorktown, was one of the heroes of that war;
and that the man he most revered, George Washington, was
first of all a soldier, that he had crossed the Delaware with
him, and, along with John Marshall, the future chief justice,

and the remnants of the army, he had been with Washington at Valley Forge during the miserable winter of 1778. Years later, in an address delivered to the Young Men's Lyceum of Springfield, Illinois, Abraham Lincoln referred to them and the other Founders as "the patriots of seventy-six."

He could not have meant they were patriots in the traditional sense; they had not fought for "their birthplace and the mansion of their fathers." They, like their fathers, had been born British subjects; they had made war on their erstwhile "British brethren," who, as they said in the Declaration of Independence, had been "deaf to the voice of justice and of consanguinity." A clue to what Lincoln meant can be found in his eulogy on Henry Clay written in 1852. Clay, he said, "loved his country partly because it was his own country, but mostly because it was a free country; and he burned with a zeal for its advancement . . . because he saw in such, the advancement, prosperity and glory, of human liberty, human right and human nature." Washington, Jefferson, Hamilton, Marshall, and the others were "the patriots of seventy-six" because, like Clay, they were devoted to the cause of human liberty, human right, and human nature, America's cause.

In speaking thus of Henry Clay, Lincoln identified what is in fact the unique character of American patriotism: the devotion not only to country (because, thanks to the Founders, there was now a country), but also to its principles, which, in our case, means the principles set down in 1776. As Thomas Pangle has rightly said, "The declaration by which Americans made themselves independent marked the birth of the first nation in history grounded explicitly not on tradition, or loyalty to tradition, but on an appeal to abstract and universal and philosophical principles of political right." Thus, while that famous American sailor Stephen Decatur thought he was being patriotic when, in 1816, he offered his toast, "Our country, may she always be in the right; but our country, right or wrong," he could be accused of being un-American, a term for which there is no counterpart in any other land or language.

Another element in American patriotism deserves to be remarked upon: devotion to a principle requires an under-standing of its terms, and, especially in the case of an ab-stract philosophical principle, that understanding cannot be taken for granted. Most people can enjoy liberty, but not everyone understands its foundation in principle. Not only that, but people can disagree as to its meaning; to be specific, not everyone agreed with Lincoln that the principles of the Declaration of Independence had been violated by congres-sional legislation allowing the people of the territories to de-cide whether to come into the Union as free or slave states, and by a Supreme Court case holding that black persons could not be citizens of the United States. (My references are, of course, to the Kansas-Nebraska Act of 1854 and to the decision in *Dred Scott* v. *Sandford* in 1857.) That disagree-ment led to civil war, with not one but both sides claiming to fight for liberty and self-government.

Furthermore, the effort to understand a principle neces-sarily requires one to consider, indeed, to question its valid-ity. Is it, in fact, true that *all* men are created equal? Did nature's God really endow everyone with the rights to life, liberty, and the pursuit of happiness? And does it follow that the purpose of government is "to secure these rights"? The patriots of seventy-six held these to be "self-evident" truths, but King George III held them to be arrogant nonsense, and, of greater consequence in our subsequent history, the vice president of the Confederate States of America held them to be self-evident lies.

It is also possible to doubt whether those principles, even if true, can provide a foundation for viable government. As I indicated in an earlier chapter, Jean-Jacques Rousseau denied that they could provide that foundation, and even Lincoln said it was problematical. To say that all men are created equal means that no man may govern another without his consent, and it is unlikely that a man will give his consent to anything other than a democratic form of government. Thus, in a 1838 speech to the Young Men's Lyceum of Springfield, Illinois, entitled, not incidentally, "The Perpetuation of Our Political Institutions," Lincoln said that the patriots of seventy-six had fought to demonstrate the truth of "a proposition, which had hitherto been considered, at best no better than problematical; namely, *the capability of a people to govern themselves*" (emphasis in original). A proposition is a statement requiring demonstration, and the proposition that people are capable of governing themselves had still to be demonstrated. This, at least, was Lincoln's view in 1838, and events leading up to the Civil War were to justify his misgivings.

Demonstration depended on the perpetuation of the institutions, and this, especially when the war came, depended on a new generation of patriots. The patriots of seventy-six were moved to do what they did by their attachment to the abstract idea (and promise) of liberty—or, to quote Alexis de Tocqueville, by their hope to "speak, live, and breathe freely, owing obedience to no authority save God and the laws of the land"—but Lincoln wondered whether those who came after them were capable of that sort of attachment. More to the point—and that point was reached in 1861—would the men of this later generation fight to preserve the institutions, founded on that principle, even as the patriots of seventy-six had fought to "ordain and establish" the institutions founded on it? In a word, would they recognize a patriotic duty to give their lives for their country? Lincoln had no way of knowing the answer to this question.

Lincoln had never held an executive office, yet the situation he faced when taking office on March 4, 1861, was fraught with danger and called for statesmanship of the highest order. He was very much aware of that. When leaving Springfield to assume the burdens of the presidency, he said his task "was greater than that which rested upon Washington," and so it was. Washington led the armed forces of a country united under the Articles of Confederation and Perpetual Union, and the Union had presumably been made "more perfect" by the Constitution of 1787, under which he took the presidential office in 1789. But when Lincoln took office, seven of the fifteen slave states, claiming both a natural and constitutional right to do so, had seceded from the Union.

The ordinance of the first state to secede read as follows:

We, the People of the State of South Carolina, in Convention assembled, do declare and ordain, and it is hereby declared and ordained,

That the Ordinance adopted by us in Convention, on the twenty-third day of May, in the year of our Lord one thousand seven hundred and eighty-eight, whereby the Constitution of the United States was ratified, and also, all Acts and parts of Acts of the General Assembly of this State, ratifying amendments of the said Constitution, are hereby repealed; and that the union now subsisting between South Carolina and other States, under the name of "The United States of America," is hereby dissolved.

Reduced to its essentials, theirs was the familiar American argument that no people may be governed without its consent, and that, naturally as well as constitutionally, they were a people capable of giving and withdrawing, or authorized to give and withdraw, their consent. Lincoln, of course, disagreed.

He began his first Inaugural Address by arguing that the southern states had no good reason to secede, and then proceeded to show that they had no right to secede, that "in contemplation of universal law, and of the Constitution, the Union of these States is perpetual." Whatever might be said of the natural right of the people of a state to do what the American people had done in 1776, they had no constitutional right to secede from the Union, or, as Lincoln put it, it is safe to assert that no government "ever had a provision in its organic law for its own termination."

He could not have believed that his argument, good as it was, would carry any weight with the likes of South Carolina and the other Deep South states. They had formed a confederacy, written a constitution, elected a congress, and, so they claimed, taken their "separate and equal place" among the nations of the earth. All Lincoln could hope to do was to persuade the other slave states not to join them, but he was limited as to what he might do or say by way of persuading them of this. He could not threaten to use force because that would almost certainly cause the other slave states to join the Confederacy; besides, with an army consisting of only some sixteen thousand men, most of them scattered in the forts and posts on the other side of the Mississippi, he had very little force to use. He hoped especially to keep the border states—Maryland and Virginia, which surrounded the capital in Washington on all four sides, as well as Delaware, Kentucky, and Missouri—in the Union, even though they were slave states. He knew (and a mere glance at the map will confirm) that in the event of war, the

Union could not be preserved if they joined the Confederacy (and only Virginia did); but he knew (and events were to confirm) that the Union probably could not be preserved without war.

So his words were addressed to the people of the border states; but not only to them. They were addressed as well to his fellow citizens in the North. He had to persuade them, as he had to persuade the others, that his purpose was peace, that he intended to do no more than what he had taken a solemn oath to do, namely, to see to it that the laws were "faithfully executed in all the States," that this was his duty, and that he would perform it, "so far as practicable, unless [his] rightful masters, the American people, shall withhold the requisite means, or, in some authoritative manner, direct the contrary." Indeed, he was speaking to the people of the northern states even when he spoke directly to the Confederates, saying that in *their* hands, not his, "is the momentous issue of civil war," that they (the Confederates) had "no oath registered in Heaven to destroy the government, while [he had] the most solemn one to 'preserve, protect and defend it.'" In saying this, he reminded his fellow citizens in the North that war was likely, even imminent, that the Union was at risk, and that they might be called on to fight for it. And throughout that address, he reminded them that the Union was a cause well worth fighting for.* Fight they did,

---

*Not everyone, not even every Republican, agreed with Lincoln on this. Horace Greeley, for example, the editor of the *New York Tribune,* probably the country's most influential newspaper, was already on record as having written that "if the Cotton States shall become satisfied that they can do better out of the Union than in it, we insist on letting them go." Greeley, the very model of a modern intellectual, fancied himself the true voice of the nation. Thus, in August 1862, in an editorial entitled "The Prayer of Twenty Millions," he chided Lincoln for his failure to emancipate the slaves; then, in July 1864 he urged him to make peace with the "Southern insurgents" without insisting on the emancipation of the slaves.

for five hard years, during which Lincoln proved to be the greatest president this country has ever had. And much of his greatness consisted in the power and beauty of his words.

It has been said that the example of Abraham Lincoln makes it possible to believe in democracy, meaning, I suppose, that if a man with his background could be elected to the highest of its offices, that is proof of the justice of democracy. His background is too well known to require a full description here, but, briefly, he was born and raised under the most unfavorable of conditions, he had little formal education, and, when a young man, he lived in New Salem, Illinois, a town with about a hundred residents, little civilization, and where he earned a living clerking in a general store.

The Springfield that he moved to, and where he began to practice law, was not much better. Yet, in both places, something drove him to get his hands on books: a grammar book, *Robinson Crusoe*, *Pilgrim's Progress*, Parson Weems's *Life of Washington*, Shakespeare's plays—his favorite was *Macbeth* ("It is wonderful," he said)—and, strangely, one might think, Euclid's *Elements*.

In those days in Illinois, judges would go on circuit, as we say, and with them would go the lawyers, moving from town to town, trying cases by day and staying in the same hotel, and frequently in the same room, by night. Lincoln's law partner, "Billy" Herndon, tells of how, while the rest of them were sleeping, sometimes in the same bed, Lincoln would lie on the floor with a lamp studying Euclid's geometry, beginning with the definition that "a point is that which has no part" and proceeding through Euclid's demonstrations, for instance, that the three angles of any triangle are equal to two right angles. There is intellectual beauty, an elegance, in the *Elements*—it is one of the Great Books and still studied where such books are part of the curriculum—still, only an unusual intellectual curiosity could have led a backwoods lawyer to pick it up and proceed to master it.

And, of course, Lincoln read the Bible. From it he got his metaphors: a house divided against itself cannot stand (from Mark 3:25); and his lessons: "Woe unto the world because of offenses! for it must needs be that offenses come; but woe to that man by whom the offense commeth" (from Matthew 18:7), and "the judgments of the Lord, are true and righteous altogether" (from Psalms 19:9); and the rhythm, the music of his language, for example, his words spoken on the railroad platform as he left for Washington to take on the burdens of the presidency: "To His care commending you, as I hope you will commend me, I bid you an affectionate farewell" (compare, in the King James version, Proverbs 30:18–19). Our politicians use the language of business ("bottom line") or sport ("the ball's in their court"), but Lincoln used the language of the Bible, in part, of course, because he was speaking to an audience that knew the Bible.

It is not strange that he should think *Macbeth* "wonderful," the greatest of Shakespeare's dramas. *Macbeth* is a play about ambition, and what ambition will lead some men to do; and we have Herndon's word for it that Lincoln was, to say the least, ambitious. In that speech to the Young Men's Lyceum—I shall say more about it in due course—he spoke of Alexander, Caesar, and Napoleon, all men of great ambition and all destroyers of republican institutions. He clearly saw himself as someone capable of being a Caesar; he, too, was a man of extraordinary ambition, extraordinary passions, extraordinary capacities (including an extraordinary intellect), and a man fully aware of his superiority, which he tried to hide by pretending to be just one of the boys who tell bawdy stories. Yet, instead of playing the role of Caesar and destroying the American Republic, he saved it. He saved it by his actions, of course, and as one of his biographers rightly says, he was the only one who could have done so; more than anyone else, he was responsible for winning the Civil War. But he also saved it, for his time and ours, with his words.

"In the beginning was the word," as we are told in the first line of John's Gospel. And in the beginning of the United States was the word, the words of the Declaration of Independence written four score and seven years before 1863, the occasion of Lincoln's words at Gettysburg. The greatest threat to the nation, as he saw it, was that Americans would cease to remember those words, cease to be devoted to the principle they expressed: that *all* men are created equal, which means that no man may rightly govern another without his consent. He put his words to the task of preventing this from happening, and he was the greatest speaker of words, the greatest orator, and, in his own way, the greatest poet this country has ever known, or is likely to know.

Most Americans—at least, this used to be the case—are somewhat aware of the power and beauty of Lincoln's words. There was a time when schoolchildren were required to memorize many of them, including, in addition to his public speeches, that famous letter to Mrs. Bixby, who, like the Spartan mother recalled by Rousseau (and Plutarch), was supposed to have lost five sons on the battlefield. Less familiar is another, and truly beautiful, letter of condolence, this one to a teenage girl, Fanny McCullough, the daughter of an Illinois friend who had been killed in action. Hearing of this, Lincoln, in the midst of all his troubles—the time was December 1862, a week before he was to issue the Emancipation Proclamation for which he was still trying to win political support, and three months after the Battle of

Antietam (the bloodiest day in American history), after which he discharged General George McClellan from command of the Army of the Potomac and replaced him with General Ambrose Burnside, who, ten days before this letter, committed the disaster of Fredericksburg—in the midst of all these troubles Lincoln wrote, in his own hand, this letter:

Dear Fanny:
It is with deep grief that I learn of the death of your kind and brave Father; and, especially, that it is affecting your young heart beyond what is common in such cases. In this sad world of ours, sorrow comes to all; and, to the young, it comes with bitterest agony, because it takes them unawares. The older have learned to ever expect it. I am anxious to afford some alleviation of your present distress. Perfect relief is not possible, except with time. You can not now realize that you will ever feel better. Is this not so? And yet it is a mistake. You are sure to be happy again. To know this, which is certainly true, will make you some less miserable now. I have had experience enough to know what I say; and you need only to believe it, to feel better at once. The memory of your dear Father, instead of an agony, will yet be a sad sweet feeling in your heart, of a purer, and holier sort than you have known before.
  Please present my kind regards to your afflicted Mother.
Your sincere friend, A. Lincoln.

Clearly, more than mere literary or epistolary skill went into the composition of this letter.

To appreciate what Lincoln achieved with his words, one has to understand the limitations on speech imposed by our principles. The First Amendment to the Constitution forbids laws attempting to enforce adherence to any religious creed. As I indicated in the second chapter, this provision, more than any other, embodies the newness of America, the first country to separate church and state. In the past, countries were said to be founded or, in one way or another, governed by gods: Minos, who gave the laws to Crete, was supposed to be the son of Zeus and Europa; Virgil tells us that Aeneas, the son of Venus, led the defeated Trojans to Italy; Sparta was given its laws by Lycurgus, who got them from the god Apollo; Romulus, the son of Mars, founded Rome; the British, from whom we gained our independence, were ruled, formally at least, by a king or queen who ruled by the grace of God (*Dei gratia, rex,* or *Dei gratia, regina*)—words, in abbreviated form, still reproduced on every British coin. Obedience to the laws was obedience to god, this god or that god, but a god. In the past, and in this way, religion was used to gain support for the laws. Our Constitution forbids this.

The principles of the Constitution are set down in the Declaration of Independence, a document that appeals to the "Laws of Nature and of Nature's God," a god who reveals himself not in the Bible but in the "book of nature," the book readable in our day by astrophysicists, and in those days by the philosophers of natural rights and Americans like Jefferson and the other "patriots of seventy-six," all men of the Enlightenment or the Age of Reason. Lincoln's task, or as he put it in the Young Men's Lyceum speech, the task of "our WASHINGTON," was to make the nation declared in 1776 an object of our passions, and, more precisely, of our love (for love is a passion, not a judgment arrived at by a process of ratiocination). This purpose is most evident in three of his speeches: the Lyceum speech, delivered when he was twenty-eight years old; the last paragraph of his First Inaugural; and, inevitably, the Gettysburg Address.

Most of the Lyceum speech was given over to a discussion of the passions and the role they play in politics. At our beginning, he said, the passions were "a pillar of our temple of liberty." For a while, the deep-rooted principle of hate and the powerful motive of revenge, instead of being turned against each other, were directed exclusively against the British nation. "And thus, from the force of circumstances, the basest principles of our nature, were either made to lie dormant, or to become the active agents in the advancement of the noblest of causes,—that of establishing and maintaining civil and religious liberty."

But that would change, Lincoln said, as the memory of the Revolution faded. For a while, for a generation, that memory was kept alive because in every family there was to be found "in the form of a father, husband, son, or a brother, a living history of the revolution, a history bearing the indubitable testimonies of its own authenticity, in the limbs mangled, in the scars of wounds received, in the midst of the scenes related." But those histories are gone, he said, and can no longer be read. "They *were* a fortress of strength, but, what invading foemen could *never do,* the silent artillery of time has done: the leveling of its walls."

At the time of the second speech, twenty-three years later, Lincoln is taking the presidential oath of office. He closed with these words, words that can be spoken only rarely in the life of a nation, and then only by a Lincoln:

I am loth to close. We are not enemies, but friends. We must not be enemies. Though passion may have strained, it must not break our bonds of affection. The mystic chords of memory, stretching from every battle-field, and patriot grave, to every living heart and hearthstone, all over this broad land, will yet swell the chorus of the Union, when again touched, as they surely will be, by the better angels of our nature.

But he had told us in the Lyceum speech that memories, even memories stretching from the graves of patriots, grow cold as they grow old, and will in time fade altogether—unless, by means of a rhetoric so powerful, or words so compelling and memorable, they could be made an imperishable part of the nation. Such words would require a special occasion, but that occasion was more than likely to present itself. For the Civil War was coming, he knew that, and with it would come more patriots' graves.

And when the occasion did present itself, Lincoln delivered the most beautiful speech in the English language—generations of schoolchildren used to commit it to memory—a speech of 272 words, delivered on a battlefield. "We are met on a great battle-field," he said at Gettysburg, to dedicate a cemetery filled with the graves of patriots.

But who were the patriots who died at Gettysburg? Did they include the soldiers of the Fifteenth and Forty-seventh Alabama regiments who made the attack on Little Round Top, arguably the decisive action in what was surely the decisive battle of the war, as well as the soldiers of the Twentieth Maine, Eighty-third Pennsylvania, and Forty-fourth New York who successfully defended it? To repeat, did they include, or was Lincoln's larger purpose to include, Confederate soldiers—who, to take them at their word, were fighting for hearth and home, *pro aris et focis,* and were led by a general (Robert E. Lee, by name) who resigned his commission in the Army of the United States because, as he said, he could not raise his hand against his birthplace, his home, and his children—as well as the soldiers fighting for the Union?

In one respect, their loyalties were American; at least, they were the sort of loyalties Tocqueville encountered in the America of the 1830s. He said Americans were more attached to their states than they were to the Union. "The Union," he writes, "is a vast body, which presents no definite object to patriotic feelings"; whereas the state "is identified with the soil; with the right of property and the domestic affections; with the recollections of the past, the labors of the present, and the hopes of the future."

Southerners referred to the Civil War as the War Between the States,* and, in every sense except the constitutional, it was that; it was certainly a war fought by the states, by which I mean the two armies (the Confederate solely and the Union mostly) consisted of units bearing the names of the states. Both armies were divided into corps, the corps into divisions, the divisions into brigades, the brigades into regiments, and the regiments were organized in and bore the names of their states, the southern as a matter of principle and the northern out of necessity. Thus, at the beginning, when Lincoln needed troops to put down the rebellion (there being, for all practical purposes, no Army of the United States), he issued a proclamation calling forth "the militia of the several States of the Union, to the aggregate number of seventy-five thousand," adding that "the details, for this object, will be immediately communicated to the State authorities through the War Department."

That number was to greatly expand,† but the "federal"

---

*An unreconstructed southerner must have designed the Marine Corps Memorial in Washington. Below the sculpture depicting the raising of the American flag on Iwo Jima's Mount Suribachi are listed all the wars and battles the Marine Corps has fought in its long and illustrious history, among them, as if the Marines had fought for the South, "The War Between the States."

†During the course of the war, a total of 2,778,304 men served in the armed forces of the United States, 359,528 of whom, or 13 percent, lost their lives. Of the soldiers, 2,494,592 were white, 178,975 were "colored," and 3,530 were from the various Indian Nations; in addition, there were 101,207 sailors and marines. See Frederick H. Dyer, *A Compendium of the War of the Rebellion* (Dayton, Ohio: Broadfoot Publishing Co., Morningside Press, 1909, 1994), vol. 1, pp. 11, 39, 760–61.

character of even the Union army was maintained throughout the war. Of the 3,559 organized military units (mostly
regiments), only 86 were regular army (mostly artillery bat-
teries), the remaining 3,473 were supplied by the states and
the District of Columbia. Accordingly, of the 195 infantry
regiments engaged on the Union side in the Battle of Antietam, all but 6 were state (and D.C.) regiments. The United
States was indeed a union of states, and, of course, a union
bitterly divided by states.

The conflict caused by that division led to the death of over
620,000 Americans, a total greater than the number killed in
all our other wars combined, and amounting to about 1.8 percent of the population in 1865. Hamilton was surely mistaken
when he suggested that Americans would not take to soldiering. These busy and presumably self-interested farmers,
storekeepers, merchants, bankers, and lawyers, North and
South, fought with a determination that astonished the Europeans who came here to report on the war; they fought
under miserable conditions, and suffered accordingly. And
so they fought and suffered at Gettysburg, where some
34,000 (17,700 Union and 16,300 Confederate, but all of
them Americans) were killed or wounded. They fought as
enemies, and no one was more determined than Lincoln to
fight the war to the end, but he never looked upon the Confederates as enemies.

As Lord Charnwood says, in what is still the best of the
Lincoln biographies, "This most unrelenting enemy to the
project of the Confederacy was the one man who had quite
purged his heart and mind from hatred or even anger to-
wards his fellow-countrymen of the South." The people of
the South, he says, came to know this in time, and their
leaders had already acknowledged it at a peace conference
as the war was drawing to an end. Meeting at Hampton
Roads, Virginia, Alexander Stephens, the vice president of

the Confederacy, said to Lincoln, "I understand, then, that you regard us as rebels, who are liable to be hanged for treason." Lincoln said that was so. "Well," said Stephens, "we supposed that would have to be your view. But, to tell you the truth, we have none of us been much afraid of being hanged with you as President." A pretty compliment, that, but well deserved. As Lincoln was to say a month later in his Second Inaugural, "Let us judge not that we be not judged." He, at least, was reluctant to judge, and he was certainly not prepared to hang Robert E. Lee, for example, or Stephens— he and Stephens had been Whig colleagues in Congress in the 1840s—or even the president of the Confederacy, Jefferson Davis. He knew that, however misguided, they, too, were Americans, and some of them were buried in the cemetery that he helped to dedicate.*

What Lincoln did at Gettysburg was to create new mystic chords, stretching from a new battlefield and new graves, to our hearts and hearthstones, *all* over this broad land, South as well as North, reminding us of the cause written in our book, the Declaration of Independence. His words touch or sound those chords in a way that no American, at least no American of my generation, can forget.† He used

---

*In May 1865, after Lincoln's assassination, Lee was indicted for treason by a federal grand jury in Norfolk. Lee contacted General Grant, and Grant immediately intervened with President Johnson. When Johnson insisted that Lee be tried, Grant said he would resign. "When can these men be tried?" asked the president. "Never," Grant replied, "unless they violate their paroles." Jean Edward Smith, now at work on a new biography of Grant, reports that Johnson realized that his administration would be helpless without Grant's support, and instructed the attorney general to have the proceedings dropped. Grant thereupon wrote Lee, assuring him that there would be no prosecution (Grant to Lee, June 20, 1865, 15 *Grant Papers*, 210–11).

Grant was equally magnanimous at Appomattox, and so was the Union army. See the appendix to this chapter.

† Garry Wills rightly says of Lincoln's address that the "power of words has rarely been given a more compelling demonstration." See his *Lincoln at Gettysburg: The Words that Remade America* (Thorndike, Me.: G. K. Hall, 1992), p. 20.

the occasion of the war to cause us to love the Union as he and Henry Clay loved it, because of what it stood for, and in the process we came to love him because he saved the Union and embodied what it stood for. Love and rational judgment are not incompatible or irreconcilable, but they are different.

That difference can be seen in the way Americans react to the inscriptions carved in the walls of the Lincoln and Jefferson Memorials. Prominent in the latter is Jefferson's famous statement, "I have sworn upon the altar of God eternal hostility against every form of tyranny over the mind of man." For that, and similar statements, Jefferson can be respected, especially by intellectuals who regard him as their benefactor because they fancy themselves his progeny. And, as Lincoln said more than once, he deserves to be honored as the principal author of the Declaration of Independence. But his words alone, even those of the Declaration, are not likely to call forth our love, either for him or for the nation he helped to found.

Now compare the Lincoln Memorial and its poignant inscriptions—the Gettysburg Address (I shall have more to say about it in the next chapter) and this final paragraph of the Second Inaugural: "With malice toward none; with charity for all; with firmness in the right, as God gives us to see the right, let us strive on to finish the work we are in; to bind up the nation's wounds; to care for him who shall have borne the battle, and for his widow, and his orphan—to do all which may achieve and cherish a just, and a lasting peace, among ourselves, and with all nations." Ordinary Americans are moved by these words, sometimes to tears; I have seen it happen. Lincoln speaks to them as only a great poet can speak, reminding them of the cause that binds the generations, that freedom is more than being left alone, that there is a price to be paid for it, and that they are indebted to those who have already paid it.

We are not accustomed to thinking of poetry as a part of politics, but many a poet has put at least some of his words to a political use. Shakespeare clearly did,* and so, in our own time did Poland's Czeslaw Milosz. As he says in an early poem, "What is poetry which does not save / Nations or people?" Thus, as I am reminded by Thomas Pangle, in 1980, at the height of the Solidarity movement, the Poles engraved these words of Milosz on a monument in the Gdansk shipyard:

> *You who wronged a simple man,*
> *Do not feel safe. The poet remembers.*
> *You kill one, but another is born*
> *The words are written down, the dead,*
> *the date.*
> *And you'd have done better with a*
> *morning dawn*
> *A rope, and a branch bowed beneath*
> *your weight.*

As Milosz is to the Poles, and Shakespeare is, or was, to the English (and Robert Burns to the Scots, Gabriele

---

*Only an Englishman with a tin ear (or flat soul) can fail to be moved by John of Gaunt's great patriotic speech in *Richard II*:

> *This royal throne of kings, this scepter'd isle,*
> *This earth of majesty, this seat of Mars,*
> *This other Eden, demi-paradise;*
> *This fortress built by Nature for herself*
> *Against infection and the hand of war;*
> *This happy breed of men, this little world;*
> *This precious stone set in the silver sea,*
> *Which serves it in the office of a wall,*
> *Or as a moat defensive to a house,*
> *Against the envy of less happy lands;*
> *This blessed plot, this earth, this realm, this*
> *England. . . . (act 2, sc. 1)*

D'Annunzio to the Italians, and Homer to the Greeks), so Lincoln is to us; he is our spokesman, our poet.

Lincoln's is obviously not the kind of speech we are accustomed to hearing from our politicians. America is, as it was supposed to be, a commercial republic, and even Lincoln could not write poetry, or sing as the poets sing, about commerce or business; business is prosaic. Poets sing of love, or God (which is why so much of the great choral music is liturgical), and sometimes of country, but not of markets, mergers, or commercial transactions. But despite our Founders' intentions, this busy nation got involved in a terrible civil war, a war over the soul of the nation, and with the war came Lincoln: statesman, poet, and, as one historian of the presidency has said (not irreverently), "the martyred Christ of democracy's passion play."

Without the war there would have been no Lincoln as we remember him, no Lincoln myth, no Lincoln Memorial, no Memorial Day—Decoration Day, when I was a boy—no parades down our main streets, in my case down Chicago's Michigan Avenue, with ever-diminishing numbers of the Illinois veterans of that war in the lead, carrying, or being helped to carry, their regimental standards, and the bands playing the "Battle Hymn of the Republic" and other martial music; and no state song that we sang in elementary school, a song commemorating the war and its leading Illinois heroes, Lincoln and generals Ulysses S. Grant and John A. Logan.*

*The song, "Illinois," was written in 1893 and made the official song of the state in 1925. Its first two verses are typical of the genre, singing of rivers and "prairies verdant growing," and the like; what makes it almost unique is its emphasis, in the last two verses, on the Civil War as the defining event in the history of the state:

> When you heard your country calling, Illinois, Illinois,
> Where the shot and shell were falling, Illinois, Illinois,
> When the Southern host withdrew,
> Pitting Gray against the Blue,

The Civil War, and the ceremonies remembering it, helped to make us patriots, and not only those of us from Illinois; this was largely Lincoln's doing.

Of course, his was not the only influence on us. In the past, we celebrated Memorial Day on May 30, whatever day of the week that happened to be, Lincoln's birthday on February 12, Washington's on the 22nd, and Independence Day, which had not yet disappeared in a three-day weekend, on July 4. Of greatest importance was the education we received in the public schools: we were taught to love our country even as we were taught reading, writing, and arithmetic.

Left out of this—not ignored but, for a long time, deliberately left out—were black Americans. Prior to the Civil War, almost all of them lived in the South, and, of them, nearly all were slaves whom, under the laws of the southern states, it was illegal to teach even to read and write. Luckily for us, one of them, Frederick Douglass, taught himself to read and write, and, as I point out in the next chapter, he proved to be their greatest spokesman, during the war and in the years following. And no one spoke more eloquently and truly of Lincoln.*

There were none more brave than you, Illinois, Illinois,
There were none more brave than you, Illinois.

Not without thy wondrous story, Illinois, Illinois,
Can be writ the nation's glory, Illinois, Illinois,
On the record of thy years,
Abra'am Lincoln's name appears,
Grant, and Logan, and our tears, Illinois, Illinois,
Grant, and Logan, and our tears, Illinois.

*For evidence of this, see Douglass's "Oration in Memory of Abraham Lincoln," delivered April 14, 1876, at the unveiling of the Freedman's Monument in Washington's Lincoln Park. The unveiling took place exactly eleven years after Lincoln's assassination; and it was altogether fitting that Douglass should be the principal speaker on the occasion, because the two of them, each in his own way but in concert, had done so much to bring about the event being celebrated, even as they were ever mindful of the work still to be done.

APPENDIX

At Appomattox, Joshua Lawrence Chamberlain—the colonel of the Twentieth Maine and the hero of Little Round Top, but now a major general—was given the honor of receiving the surrender of the Confederate infantry led, on this occasion, by Major General John B. Gordon. But I shall let Chamberlain's biographer tell the story (see Willard M. Wallace, *Soul of the Lion: A Biography of General Joshua L. Chamberlain* [Gettysburg, Pa.: Stan Clark Military Books, 1988], pp. 188–89, 200):

———

"Presently Gordon and the head of the leading division column—in this instance, the old Stonewall Brigade—drew almost abreast of the little knot of Union officers under the flags. Chamberlain turned and spoke a word to a man at his side. Instantly, a bugle call rang out, and the entire 1st Division of the Fifth Corps, regiment by regiment in succession, brought its muskets from 'order arms' to 'carry arms,' the marching salute.

"Gordon was riding erect, but with his chin on his chest and his eyes on the ground. As he heard the call and the machine-like shift of arms, he looked up, startled. Then he caught the significance of the movement, and his whole attitude changed. Wheeling his horse toward Chamberlain, he touched the animal slightly with the spur so that it reared, and as the horse's head came down in a graceful bow, Gordon brought his sword-point down to his boot-toe. Then wheeling back to his own column, he gave the command to carry arms. The two armies thus accorded each other the final recognition of gallant opponents. But, said Chamberlain, 'On our part not a sound of trumpet more, nor roll of drum; not a cheer, nor word nor whisper of vain-glory, nor motion of man standing again at the order, but an awed stillness rather, and breath-holding, as if it were the passing of the dead!' . . .

"Small wonder that an incident like this should have been repeated all over the South and that Gordon, who became a remarkably effective and popular public speaker in the post-war years, should time and again allude in the highest terms to Chamberlain, whom he called, 'One of the knightliest soldiers of the Federal army.' "

Chamberlain had been a Bowdoin College professor, and, after the war, was four times elected governor of Maine. He later became president of Bowdoin and died of his wartime wounds in 1914.

"WHAT COUNTRY
HAVE I?"

I have no love for America, as such; I have no patriotism.
I have no country. What country have I?

Frederick Douglass, speech before the American Anti-Slavery Society, May 11, 1847

Why, indeed, should Frederick Douglass have been a patriot? What country had he or any other Negro of his day? Why should any of them have had a love for America? Good questions, these, and some Negroes (now African Americans), and even some whites, have continued to ask them.

Thus, on June 14, 1997 (Flag Day), in what the White House said would be a "major" speech, President Bill Clinton asked whether we could "define what it means to be an American," and called for "a great and unprecedented conversation about race." Then, to help us talk about it (as if we have not been talking about it since time out of mind), he appointed a seven-member advisory panel headed by a distinguished black historian, John Hope Franklin.

Nothing came of this, partly because nothing was intended to come of it. We did not have to be told what it means to be an American, or that black Americans have been treated unjustly, especially in our beginning. Even so, Franklin was not the man to make this obvious point, not if we take him at his word. Justice for us, at least in this context, is defined by the Declaration of Independence, but, except that he called it "a tragically flawed revolutionary document," Franklin's understanding of the Declaration is indistinguishable from that of the slaveholders. It did not apply to blacks, he says; they were not, or were not thought to be, among those men whom the Creator endowed with "certain unalienable Rights." But this is what the Confederates said to justify their defense of slavery: blacks have no rights, and they cannot complain if they are treated accordingly. Chief Justice Taney made this point in his opinion for the Court in the 1857 case *Dred Scott* v. *Sandford,* and he drew the following conclusion. "Negroes have no rights," he said, or none that "the white man was bound to respect." It followed that they might "justly and lawfully" be enslaved, and, whether enslaved or freed, they were not and could not be American citizens. This decision was one of the causes of the Civil War.

As I shall point out, Frederick Douglass had a truer understanding of the Founding principles. He said he had no love for America "as such," or as it was in 1847, but he had a great love of America as those principles intended it to be. To make it so required not only the abolition of slavery and a new constitutional definition respecting citizenship, but, as Abraham Lincoln said at Gettysburg, "a new birth of freedom," and this, in turn, required a change in public sentiment. White Americans, North as well as South, had to recognize black Americans as their fellow citizens, and, as Douglass never tired of saying, it was incumbent upon his fellow blacks to demonstrate that they deserved to be treated as citizens. To this end, he urged them, among other things, to enlist in the Union army. He said that by fighting the battles of America, they could rightly claim America as their country and, moreover, "have that claim respected." And fight they did, in large numbers, and large numbers died in the fighting; but it is only in our own time, after many another war, that it can be said that Douglass was right about what they might gain by their military service. Unfortunately, he did not live to see it.

———

Douglass was born a slave on a plantation in eastern Maryland, where, not atypically, he was ill-fed and ill-clothed, and occasionally beaten for offenses that slave children were wont to commit—for example, "stealing" fruit from a garden—or were accused of having committed. He had two sisters and one brother who lived on the same plantation, but, as he said, "the early separation of us from our mother had well nigh blotted the fact of our relationship from our memories." Like others born in bondage, he had no knowledge of when he was born. As he wrote in an account of his early life, he could not remember ever having met a slave who could tell when he was born. "They seldom came nearer to it than planting-time, harvest-time, cherry-time, spring-time, or fall-time," he writes.

Then, still a young boy—he thought he may have been between seven and eight years old—he was sent by his master to Baltimore, where it was his good (and most unusual) fortune to serve a mistress who began to teach him how to read. Upon learning of this, her husband at once forbade her to continue, telling her that, in addition to being unlawful, it was "unsafe" to teach a slave to read. "If you teach that nigger how to read," he said, "there would be no keeping him." But what the woman had begun, Douglass managed to continue on his own: he learned how to read and write, and there was, indeed, no keeping him.

After being sold and resold, hired out for wages he earned but could not keep, beaten with clubs (and fighting back with his fists), on September 3, 1838, being (perhaps) twenty-one years old, he escaped his bondage in Maryland for New York City and then New Bedford, Massachusetts. There, after working as a common laborer for three years, he launched the career that was to make him a leader of the Abolitionist movement and eventually, as someone has rightly said, "without question one of the great men of his generation." A great man and a great American. His home in Washington, Cedar Hill, where he died in 1895, is now a National Historical Site, administered by the National Park Service.

But much was to happen to him before he attained that lofty status. In 1845, by publishing the narrative I have been quoting, he disclosed his whereabouts to his owner back in Maryland, and to avoid recapture—in the eyes of our law, he was, of course, still a slave—he went to England and Ireland. Or, as he puts it, "I went to England, monarchical England, to get rid of Democratic Slavery."* There was liberty in England, he said, not only for the white man, but also for him and other black men; whereas in democratic America, except in antislavery circles, he was not recognized as a man.

*He became legally "rid" of it when British friends arranged to purchase him from his Maryland owner for the sum of $711.66 (or 150 British pounds).

"I am not thought of, or spoken of, except as a piece of property belonging to some *Christian* slaveholder, and all the religious and political institutions of this country, alike pronounce me a slave and a chattel."

There is, of course, much truth in this, but, as Douglass himself was to acknowledge later on, it is not the whole truth. Opinion in the South was to change for the worse, but at our beginning even the slaveholders knew that blacks were men. Thomas Jefferson, for example, although suspecting that blacks were "inferior to the whites in the endowments both of body and mind," knew very well that they were being denied their rights as men and that this could not continue forever. He feared a slave uprising, and in that event, he said, God would be on the side of the slaves. "The Almighty has no attribute which can take side with us in such a contest."

It might be said that Jefferson was not a typical slaveholder, that, as the principal author of the Declaration of Independence, he had to know that "all men" meant *all* men, and could only mean *all* men, because there is no respect in which men are equal except in their possession of unalienable rights; nature did not create them equally white, intelligent, strong, energetic, or handsome, and they are not equally Anglo-Saxon. But Jefferson's views on this subject were by no means atypical; from the beginning and continuing well into the nineteenth century, the injustice of slavery was recognized in the South as well as in the North, and nowhere more than in the southern courts, where the humanity of the slave was acknowledged, and under the circumstances had to be acknowledged. A couple of early state cases can serve as examples.

The question in *The State of Mississippi* v. *Isaac Jones* (1820) was whether (there being no statute covering the matter) the killing of a slave (unlike the killing of, for example, a horse) was murder under the common law, which defined murder as the taking of the life of a "reasonable creature" with malice aforethought. The court held that it was and pointed out that this was the usual view of all the southern courts that had considered the question. The judge said, "At a very early period in Virginia, the [master's] power of life over slaves was given by statute, but . . . as soon as these statutes were repealed, it was at once considered by their courts, that the killing of a slave might be murder." He went on to say that slaves were persons, that the Constitution of the United States expressly designates them as persons, that the Mississippi legislature considered slaves as "reasonable and accountable beings," and that it would be a stigma on the character of the state, and a reproach to its administration of justice, if the life of a slave could be taken with impunity, "or if he could be murdered in cold blood, without subjecting the offender to the highest penalty known to the criminal jurisprudence of the country." The slave, he continued, "is still a human being, and possesses all those rights, of which he is not deprived by the positive provisions of the law."

In *State* v. *Hoover* (1839) a North Carolina court went further when it held that a master might be convicted of murder for the killing of one of his own slaves. "It must indeed be true," the judge said, "that a killing by the owner may be extenuated by many circumstances . . . but it is almost self-evident that this [owner] can claim no extenuation of his guilt." Nor, he went on, was it necessary to prove that the owner had intended to kill the slave. "If great bodily harm be intended, and that can be gathered from the nature of the means used or other circumstances, and death ensue, the party will be guilty of murder, although he may not have intended death."

There are other such cases, but, to make the point that Douglass was mistaken, or at least exaggerating, when he said that *none* of the institutions of this country recognized the humanity of a black person, it suffices to say that, just as a black person could be the victim of a crime, so, too, as a rational and morally responsible human being, could he commit a crime and be a witness to a crime, which is to say, testify to it in a court of law (see the 1849 case *State of North Carolina* v. *Caesar*).

Viewed from the perspective of the Founding generation, these decisions were not exceptional. Slavery was seen as the exception, and the Founders did what they could to keep it so. For example, when drafting the Articles of Confederation in 1778, the Continental Congress refused to allow the word "white" to be inserted into the provision, "the free [white] inhabitants of each state, paupers, vagabonds and fugitives from Justice excepted, shall be entitled to all privileges and immunities of free citizens in the several states"; and, again in 1787, in the famous Ordinance providing for the governing of the Northwest Territory, the same Congress provided that "there shall be neither slavery nor involuntary servitude in the said territory," the only negative vote being cast by one of the three New York delegates. This provision was reenacted by the new Congress of the United States in 1789, and, so far as we know, no one, in either House or Senate, not even a member from a southern state, objected.

This is not the place to deal at length with the three constitutional provisions having to do with slavery, but the one on the slave trade (Article 1, section 9) deserves at least a cursory treatment.* It reads as follows: "The Migration or Importation of such Persons as any of the States now exist-

---

*For a fuller analysis of the clause, see Walter Berns, "The Constitution and the Migration of Slaves," *Yale Law Journal* (December 1968).

ing shall think proper to admit, shall not be prohibited by the Congress prior to the Year one thousand eight hundred and eight, but a Tax or duty may be imposed on such Importation, not exceeding ten dollars for each Person."

This was, of course, a concession to the slave states, but the provision tells us something of importance about the Founders' views on the slave trade and on slavery itself, as well. In the first place, it should be noted that, in its form, this provision is not a guarantee of a right but, rather, a postponement of Congress's power to prohibit. Then, only the states originally existing were permitted to continue to import slaves—in the event, this meant Georgia and South Carolina—and this permission was limited to twenty years, after which the foreign slave trade might be (and in fact was) prohibited. Indeed, it was prohibited before 1808 when Congress organized the Mississippi Territory out of Georgia's western lands. Nor can there be any doubt as to why this temporary restriction on Congress's power (to regulate commerce) was itself restricted to the states originally existing. Clearly, the Framers intended to enable Congress to prevent the spread of slavery beyond the boundaries of the original thirteen states. As one of them said, the slave trade was a "nefarious" business, and, according to James Madison, slavery itself was a form of "barbarism."

It has become the custom, especially in academic circles, to denounce the Founders as hypocrites, who spoke ill of slavery but did nothing to put an end to it. Yet, it should be noted that no form of the word "slave" appears in their Constitution—in each case, the word employed is "person" or "persons"—and no one understood the significance of this better than Frederick Douglass. The following statement comes from an 1863 speech in which Douglass called for the enlistment of "colored" troops:

I hold that the Federal Government was never, in its essence, anything but an anti-slavery government. Abolish slavery to-morrow, and not a sentence or syllable of the Constitution need be altered. It was purposely so framed as to give no claim, no sanction to the claim, of property in a man. If in its origin slavery had any relation to the government, it was only as the scaffolding to the magnificent structure, to be removed as soon as the building was completed.

By "scaffolding," Douglass meant the three constitutional provisions addressed to the slavery question: the provision in Article 1, section 2(3), whereby the southern states were allowed to count three of their five slaves for purposes of representation in the House of Representatives; the one in Article 1, section 9, allowing them, for twenty years, to import more slaves from abroad; and, finally, the one in Article 4, section 2(3), providing for the return of fugitive slaves. These concessions to slavery, demanded by the southern states, were the original price of union, and the Framers did indeed pay that price—and to this day have been criticized for doing so—but they paid it grudgingly, out of what they thought was necessity. Anyone who says the price was too high is obliged to demonstrate that the lot of the slaves would have been better if the southern states had been allowed to form (as in 1860–61 they did form) their own confederation.*

---

*That case has been argued, but not persuasively. The slaves would have remained slaves in the South, and, assuming the northern states would have done then what they did in fact do on the eve of the Civil War, Negroes (freed or fugitives) would not have been welcomed in the North. In fact, they would have been forbidden to enter or remain in any of the contiguous states. Here are the relevant provisions in the Indiana constitution of 1851: "No negro or mulatto shall come into, or settle in the State, after the adoption of this constitution." And, "All contracts made with any negro or mulatto coming into the State, contrary to the pro-

But by 1847, when Douglass was moved to say that he had no patriotism because he had no country, the situation of the slave had become worse, not better. By this time no one had reason to hope, as the Founders had hoped, that slavery had been put on a path leading to its ultimate extinction. Rather than being confined to the states originally existing, slavery had been allowed to spread westward. Missouri had been allowed to come into the Union as a slave state (albeit only after an acrimonious debate extending over the better part of two years); the country had made war on Mexico, and the southerners, who had agreed in 1820 to exclude slavery from those parts of the Louisiana Territory north of Missouri, succeeded in preventing the adoption of the resolution (the so-called Wilmot Proviso) that, if adopted, would have kept it out of the territory acquired from Mexico. They went so far as to challenge the constitutionality of the Wilmot Proviso, claiming that Congress had no power to exclude slavery from a territory, which, as I pointed out above, Congress had done from the beginning—and done without opposition from its southern members.

Douglass would have even greater reason to despair as the 1840s gave way to the 1850s. In 1854 Congress passed the Kansas-Nebraska Act, repealing the Missouri Compromise law and allowing the people of the territories to decide for themselves whether to come into the Union as free or slave states. Free of the stigma the Founders had explicitly as well as implicitly attached to it, slavery was now seen as a matter of no great significance, a matter to be decided by a majority vote of the (white) people immediately involved—which

---

visions of the foregoing section, shall be void: and any person who shall employ such negro or mulatto, or otherwise encourage him to remain in the State, shall be fined in any sum not less than ten dollars, nor more than five hundred dollars." Ohio, Illinois, and Iowa had similar provisions.

Lincoln rightly saw as a repudiation of the Declaration of Independence. Tellingly, the author and chief proponent of this measure was not a southerner; he was Stephen A. Douglas of Illinois.

Worse was still to come. In 1857 the Supreme Court of the United States handed down its infamous decision in the case *Dred Scott* v. *Sandford*. In addition to deciding the narrow issue coming to it from the lower federal court,* the Court declared the Missouri Compromise (already repealed by the Kansas-Nebraska Act) unconstitutional on the ground that, by prohibiting slavery in a territory, the 1820 law deprived a slaveholder of his property without due process of law. According to the Court, there was no difference between property in a slave or in a bale of cotton. As if this were not enough of a departure from the original understanding, the Court, speaking through Chief Justice Roger B. Taney (of Maryland, and a Jacksonian Democrat), went on to say that "the property in a slave is distinctly and expressly affirmed in the Constitution." Nothing, of course,

---

*Scott was a slave owned by a Doctor Emerson, an army surgeon, and taken by him from Missouri (a slave state) to Illinois (a free state) and then to Fort Snelling in what is now Minnesota, but at the time was part of the Louisiana Territory, where, under the Missouri Compromise of 1820, slavery was forbidden. On their return to Missouri, Emerson died and Scott tried to purchase his freedom from Mrs. Emerson. Failing in this, he sued for his freedom in the Missouri court, claiming that he had become free while a resident in Illinois and the Louisiana Territory, and that, citing the principle "once free, always free," which had been the rule in most southern courts, he remained a free man on his return to Missouri. Scott won in the lower court, but the decision was reversed on appeal. On Mrs. Emerson's remarriage, Scott became the property of her brother, John Sandford, a citizen of New York, which enabled Scott to sue in a federal court under the provision of the Constitution that gives federal courts jurisdiction in cases between citizens of different states. Thus, the narrow issue in the case was whether Scott was, as he claimed, a citizen of Missouri. The Supreme Court held that because he was a Negro, and even if he were a free Negro, he was not and could not be "a citizen of a state in the sense in which that word is used [in the Constitution]."

could be further from the truth. As Herbert Storing says, "If one had to think of two adverbs that do *not* describe the way the Constitution acknowledged slavery, he could not do better than 'distinctly' and 'expressly.' " And if, on the eve of the Civil War, someone had asked Frederick Douglass why he could not be a patriot, he could not have done better than to point to *Dred Scott* v. *Sandford* and the state case that followed it, *Mitchell* v. *Nancy Wells*.

Earlier in this chapter I made much of the fact that even in Mississippi a slave was recognized as a human being who possesses all those natural rights "of which he is not deprived by the positive provisions of the law." That was in 1820; in 1859 the Mississippi High Court of Errors and Appeals held that a slave, or even a former slave, had no rights whatsoever, that, quoting Taney's opinion in *Dred Scott,* Negroes were "an inferior class of beings." (I note, but only in passing, that the slaveholder whose actions gave rise to this case could not have shared this opinion.)

Nancy Wells was the daughter of a female slave and a white slaveholder named Edward Wells. In 1846 her father took her, then a child, to Ohio, where he provided for her care, and where she was free under the laws of that state. He died in 1848; under the terms of his will, she was to receive a gold watch, a bed, and $3,000. Mitchell, the executor of the father's estate, refused to give her the legacy, and in 1857 she brought this suit.

As the court saw it, the issue was simple enough: was she, a citizen of Ohio, entitled to sue in the Mississippi court? The court, with one judge dissenting, held that she was not. Speaking for the majority, a Judge Harris acknowledged that, under the doctrine of comity, citizens of other states were allowed to bring actions in the courts of Mississippi, and he acknowledged that Ohio recognized her as a citizen;

but he said that Mississippi was not required to do so. Ohio, he said, not only claimed the right to degrade and disgrace herself and, by doing so, wrong the state of Mississippi, but also claimed "that she [Ohio] has the right to force her new associate into the Mississippi branch of the American family, to claim and exercise rights *here,* which our laws have always denied this inferior race, and that Mississippi is bound to yield obedience to such demand." He thought this demand outrageous.

Suppose that Ohio, still further afflicted with her peculiar philanthropy, should determine to descend another grade in the scale of her peculiar humanity, and claim to confer citizenship on the chimpanzee or the ourang-outang (the most respectable of the monkey tribe), are we to be told that "comity" will require of the States not demented, to forget their own policy and self-respect, and lower their own citizens and institutions in the scale of being, to meet the necessities of the mongrel race thus attempted to be introduced into the family of sisters in this confederacy?

Judge Harris's statement may have been unusually nasty—one may doubt that its like can be found even in the reports of South African courts during the apartheid era—but there was nothing unusual about his views on slavery; in fact, within two years those views were given official status in the Confederate constitution.

In a major speech on that constitution, delivered at Savannah, Georgia, on March 21, 1861, Alexander Stephens, the vice president of the Confederate States of America, admitted that the "prevailing ideas entertained by [Thomas Jefferson] and most of the leading statesmen at the time of the formation of the [Constitution of the United States], were that the enslavement of the African was in violation of the laws of nature: that it was wrong in principle, socially, morally, and politically." But, unlike Lincoln, who made the same point in his opening lines at Gettysburg, Stephens said these original ideas had been shown to be wrong, fundamentally wrong. "They rested upon the assumption of the equality of the races," but further developments in the realm of science had shown this to be "an error." The new Confederate government, he said, is founded upon exactly the opposite idea:

Its foundations are laid, its corner stone rests upon the great truth that the negro is not equal to the white man. That slavery—subordination to the superior race, is his natural and normal condition. This, our new Government, is the first, in the history of the world, based upon this physical and moral truth.

Opinions like these, especially opinions claiming the authority of science, are not readily changed; yet they would have to be changed if, as Lincoln said at Gettysburg, this nation was to have a "new birth of freedom."

One of the many striking things about the Gettysburg Address is the term Lincoln used when speaking of the United States. His practice had been to speak of the "Union"—twenty times in the First Inaugural, for example, thirty-two times in his Message to Congress on July 4, 1861 (and nine times in that famous letter to Horace Greeley where he said his primary purpose was to save the Union)—and only rarely of the "nation." Yet, at Gettysburg, he spoke five times of the "nation" and not once of the "Union." (The full text of the Gettysburg Address is reprinted at the end of this chapter in the appendix.) In a speech so carefully crafted, this could not have been unintentional or inadvertent. He spoke of the nation because what he had to say was addressed to the people constituting the nation, South as well as North.

The South insisted that the United States was a union of states, not of people, and despite every word Lincoln had addressed to the states (or their representatives) on those earlier occasions, some of them had seceded; and he had to know that nothing he could say would bring them back. Not in principle—on this Lincoln was adamant—but in fact the Union had ceased to exist; and the rupture of the Union had been caused by a division in the nation. The nation was no longer what both Lincoln and Alexander Stephens agreed that it had been four score and seven years earlier, namely, as Lincoln put it, a "new nation," brought forth on this continent by "our fathers," our *common* fathers, and "conceived in Liberty, and dedicated to the proposition that all men are created equal." Where then there had been one nation, united in its dedication to that proposition, there were now two, and Lincoln's immediate purpose was to repair that division.

Now obviously, when he referred to those who had given their lives at Gettysburg "that that nation might live," he could not have meant to include the Confederates who had given their lives that that nation might die. Here he was speaking of the Union dead, but, as he said, their work was "unfinished." What remained to be done—"the great task remaining before us"—could only be done by "the living," and the living had to include the southern people; without them, and without their *freely* given consent, that work could not be finished. They, too, had to highly resolve that this nation "shall have a new birth of freedom—and that government of the people, by the people, for the people, shall not perish from the earth." They, too, were his audience at Gettysburg.

To be more precise, southerners had not only to learn to live without slavery, but—and this applied as well to the people of the North—they had to recognize the former slaves as their fellow citizens. In a legal sense, the former slaves could be made citizens by constitutional amendment—the Fourteenth, as it happened—and, by making it a condition of their being represented again in the House and Senate, the southern states could be made to ratify that amendment; but what remained to be done could not be done by adding words to the Constitution. Lincoln knew that; as he said in 1858, public sentiment is "everything" in a democracy. If so, what was required before this nation could have a new birth of freedom was a change in public sentiment. Without that change, blacks would continue to be seen by whites as a separate people, and by themselves as a people without a country.

Although his assassination in April 1865 meant that the task of effecting this change would fall into other hands, Lincoln had given more than a little thought to the problems it posed. To judge from his efforts in the case of Louisiana, a significant part of which had, early in the war, come under the control of Union forces, his policy on reconciliation or reconstruction (as it came to be called) would be governed by the same principle that governed his earlier efforts to effect an abolition of slavery, namely, that the desired action would be better done if it were done by the southern people themselves, and that it would be more likely to be done by them if they were permitted to do it gradually and at the least possible cost to them.*

*In his Annual Message to Congress of December 1, 1862, Lincoln called upon Congress to propose a constitutional amendment whereby the government would provide compensation, in the form of government bonds, to any state that should abolish slavery before January 1, 1900, the amount of compensation to de-

Accordingly, on December 8, 1863, less than three weeks after the Gettysburg Address, Lincoln issued a proclamation outlining his amnesty and reconstruction policy. Generally, it provided that whenever a state should reestablish a government—favored by voters "no less than one-tenth in number of the votes cast in such State at the [1860] Presidential election," each voter having taken an oath to support the Constitution of the United States and all acts of Congress and proclamations by the president favoring the abolition of slavery—such should be recognized as the true government of the state. Beyond this, the proclamation called upon the states to recognize and declare the "permanent" freedom of the former slaves, to "provide for their education" and (recognizing their "present condition as a laboring, landless, and homeless class") a system of apprenticeships.

According to the 1860 census, there were 350,000 blacks in Louisiana, or almost 50 percent of the total state population; of that number most were freed by the Emancipation Proclamation of January 1, 1863, but they resided in that part of the state not yet controlled by Union forces (all of Louisiana outside New Orleans and nearby "parishes," or counties).* Of the whites, even those living in the environs

---

pend on the number of slaves freed. Nothing came of this plan, but, as he pointed out, there was much to be said in its favor. Among its other advantages, it would, he said, spare "both races from the evils of sudden derangement." Lincoln's prescience was confirmed after the war by Frederick Douglass. Surveying the effects of "sudden derangement," he wrote that the Negro was "free from the individual master but a slave of society. He had neither money, property, nor friends. He was free from the old plantation, but he had nothing but the dusty road under his feet. . . . He was turned loose naked, hungry, and destitute to the open sky." Foreseeing this, Lincoln had hoped to prevent it.

*The Emancipation Proclamation abolished slavery in those states, and parts of states, then in rebellion against the United States. It was so limited because Lincoln's authority to issue it derived from his power as commander-in-chief of the army and navy.

of New Orleans, most were pro-Confederacy, and of the pro-Unionists, some were opposed to abolition and, judging by the election results, most were opposed to black suffrage. This was the situation Lincoln (and after him, Congress) had to contend with.

Even so, after a struggle lasting well over a year, on September 5, 1864, a new Louisiana constitution was adopted providing for the abolition of slavery, the public education of black children between the ages of six and eighteen years, the enlistment of black men in the state militia, and the right of blacks to appeal to the courts for a redress of any injuries done to their lands, goods, persons, or reputations. But, despite Lincoln's appeal that, at least, "the very intelligent, and especially those who have fought gallantly in our ranks," be given the right to vote, the new constitution provided no guarantee of black suffrage. The best that Lincoln and his agents on the scene could achieve was a provision giving the legislature the authority to enfranchise non-whites on the basis of military service, taxation, or intellectual fitness. According to the best account we have of these events, it is possible that had he lived, Lincoln's efforts to get the Louisiana legislature to exercise this power might have succeeded.

And it is not impossible that, had he lived, he might have succeeded in getting Congress to recognize the new government of Louisiana by allowing its members to take their seats in the House and Senate. As it happened, that issue, although long debated, was not decided until after his death, and the man who succeeded him, Andrew Johnson, not only lacked his political skills and finesse, but suffered from the fact that he was a Democrat—a Union Democrat, to be sure (which is why he was put on the ticket with Lincoln in 1864), but still a Democrat—at a time when Congress was controlled by Republicans. Johnson made an attempt (for a while) to carry out Lincoln's policy, but any possibility that Reconstruction would follow the path Lincoln had prescribed for Louisiana was doomed when the new governments in the South, although ratifying the Thirteenth Amendment (which abolished slavery) and repudiating the Confederate war debts, passed a series of so-called black codes imposing restrictions on the freedmen. These codes varied in harshness, but in no state were blacks allowed to vote or serve on juries. This was enough to ensure that Congress, not the president, and especially not a president like Andrew Johnson, would be in charge of Reconstruction and that its terms would be largely defined by the Radical Republicans, who, while he lived, were inclined to oppose even Lincoln.

They divided the South into five military districts, each commanded by a major general given the task of enforcing the newly enacted legislation guaranteeing the political and civil rights of the former slaves. Imposed on a people accustomed to governing themselves, this program, not surprisingly, was met with resistance. Furthermore, even under the most propitious of circumstances, there are limits to what an occupying army might do. It might, as it did, protect the right of blacks to vote and to hold public office; and it might, as it did, maintain public order by arresting those who threatened it; but it could not ensure that those arrested would be indicted or, if indicted, that a local jury would vote to convict them. And its numbers were too few to put down resistance when it became violent.*

---

*That an army might be employed in a successful effort to change opinion was demonstrated in the 1950s and '60s, first at Little Rock, Arkansas, and then at the University of Mississippi. I was witness to one event in this "second Reconstruction," as it has been called. In the spring of 1956, two years after the Supreme

Historians disagree as to whether, had the congressional Republicans persisted, Radical Reconstruction (as it came to be called) might have succeeded, and southerners might have learned not only to live without slavery but to recognize the former slaves as their fellow citizens. But in time, and with an increase in the number of Democrats in Congress, support for the program waned; and in 1877—probably as a result of a bargain allowing the Republican Rutherford B. Hayes to be declared the winner in the disputed presidential election—the last of the federal troops were withdrawn from the South. Their departure marked the end of Reconstruction. As C. Vann Woodward puts it, in 1877 the rest of the country acquiesced in the South's demand that "the whole problem be left to the disposition of the dominant Southern white people." So much for Lincoln's hope that the nation might have a new birth of freedom.

What followed—not immediately but perhaps inevitably—were segregation statutes, or "Jim Crow" laws, that ostracized blacks from southern society, an ostracism, similar in every respect to South Africa's apartheid, that extended to churches and schools, housing and jobs, eating and drinking, trains and buses, sports and recreation, hospitals and orphanages, prisons and asylums, and ultimately, as Woodward says, "to funeral homes, morgues, and cemeteries." By the turn of the century, blacks could no longer vote,

---

Court's decision in the school segregation case, I had an appointment with the president of Louisiana State University, Troy Middleton, a retired army general who, during World War II, had commanded the Eighth Corps of General George Patton's Third Army. Sitting in his outer office, I could hear snatches of a heated conversation taking place inside. Finally, I heard Middleton say, in a loud voice, accompanied by a rhythmic pounding of his desk, "Forty years ago [bang] I took an oath to support and defend the Constitution of the United States [bang] against all enemies, foreign and domestic [bang], and, by God [bang], I intend to do so!" A mere assistant professor of political science at the time, I was impressed.

hold office, serve on juries, or be represented in local councils, state legislatures, or the national Congress. Almost two hundred thousand of them had fought for the Union in the Civil War, of whom 33,665 died, and this was their reward.

No one had greater reason to be saddened by this than Frederick Douglass, because no one was more insistent that they serve and fight. By serving, he said, they could send a needed message to their enemies, the "Negro-hater and slavery-lover"; they could learn the use of arms and how to defend themselves; and, most of all, they could earn the right to be treated as men and citizens. "Once let the black man get upon his person the brass letters U.S.; let him get an eagle on his button, and a musket on his shoulder, and bullets in his pocket, and there is no power on the earth or under the earth which can deny that he has earned the right of citizenship in the United States."

Blacks did become citizens—or better, their citizenship was confirmed—in 1868 with the adoption of the Fourteenth Amendment. And they have long enjoyed at least one of the rights of citizens, namely, the right to bear arms, but, until recently, not in the company of their white fellow citizens. In the Civil War, and after it in Texas and the Indian Territory (where they gained a measure of fame as "Buffalo Soldiers"), in the Philippines and Cuba during the Spanish-American War, and finally in the two world wars, they did their fighting in all-black units.* This began to change when, in 1948, President Harry Truman signed an executive order requiring the military to desegregate "as rapidly as possible."

---

*Their lot was somewhat different in the navy. Like every sailor and officer, they were assigned a battle station, but beyond that, as I can attest, their job was to wait on tables in the officers' wardroom, make their beds, clean their rooms and (in naval parlance) their "heads." In a word, they were servants.

The status of blacks in the military was further affected by the Vietnam War. In the first place, they (like whites) could no longer be drafted. In 1973 President Richard Nixon abolished conscription (unpopularly known as the draft) in favor of an all-volunteer military. Secondly, the unpopularity of that war had an effect on the army itself; at its conclusion, it was a discredited institution. The best of its officers and enlisted men left the service in record numbers, and those recruited to replace them, whites and blacks alike, came from the underclass. This, we are told, had two consequences, both of them affecting blacks, and one of them happy. The first was racial strife. Already common enough in Southeast Asia, "racial strife reached epidemic proportions," especially among the troops stationed in Germany. The happy consequence was a "transformed" army, in which blacks constitute 27 percent of all personnel, 35 percent of noncommissioned officers (corporals and sergeants), and 12 percent of commissioned officers (lieutenants up to and including generals). And there are no all-black units.

It is, in fact, a thoroughly integrated army. Enlisted men, blacks and whites, live in the same barracks, eat in the same mess halls (now called dining facilities), and, although not required to do so, at the same tables, something rarely encountered in our universities. The army does not claim to be colorblind; it takes account of race, it even counts by race, but, unlike the Department of Justice, not with the view to separating the races. (There is nothing like a gerrymandered voting district in the army.) On the contrary, the army sees to it that every platoon consists of both blacks and whites, and that a company commanded by a white officer will have a black first sergeant, and one commanded by a black officer, a white first sergeant.

The army has its race problems, but, in the opinion of the soldiers, blacks as well as whites, race relations are better in the army than in the wider society, better by far than in the universities. Both are under political pressure to practice affirmative action, universities when admitting students and hiring professors and the army when promoting officers; but the army does this without lowering standards. Unlike the universities or, for that matter, the civil service, it cannot do otherwise; after all, while it is obliged to avoid discrimination, its chief obligation is to be an effective fighting force, and the army is ever mindful of this. Its policy is to promote blacks at a rate not less than the rate at which whites are promoted, but the rate, whatever it is, is based not on the numbers of whites and blacks in the army, but, rather, on their numbers among those determined to be eligible for promotion. Obviously, much depends on how eligibility is determined, but, on this score, the army seems to do better than other institutions.

As one might expect, there are whites who complain of reverse discrimination, but such cases must be few in number because, according to one authoritative study, "the Army is the only place in American life where whites are routinely bossed around by blacks," and, apparently, without the whites resenting it.* And there are also blacks who claim to be victims of discrimination, which, despite the army's efforts to eliminate it, almost surely continues to exist to some extent and in one form or another. In the blunt words of one senior black officer, "You don't have to be supernigger any more, but you still have to be better than the rest to make it." Those who are passed over might have reason to complain,

*Charles C. Moskos and John Sibley Butler, *All that We Can Be: Black Leadership and Racial Integration the Army Way* (New York: A Twentieth Century Fund Book, Basic Books, 1996), p. 2.

but, as a retired black general said, "by their paying the penalty, it meant that those of us who made it were never looked upon as beneficiaries of racial favoritism." The importance of this cannot be exaggerated. Unlike the student admitted (or the professor hired) under a quota system, these black officers are free of the stigma attached to affirmative action. Their pride is intact.

This, and much more in the army today, goes far to justify Frederick Douglass's advice to the black men of his day. Enlist for your own sake, he said to them. "You will stand more erect, walk more assured, feel more at ease, and be less liable to insult than you ever were before." Enlist not only for the sake of your pride, he said, but because the man "who fights the battles of America may claim America as his country—and have that claim respected." There may have once been doubts about this, but, to judge from what was said by the African Americans immediately involved in it, these doubts were resolved by the time of the Gulf War.

Shortly after the conclusion of the ground war, a number of these African Americans were interviewed in Saudi Arabia by a woman reporter for the *MacNeil-Lehrer News Hour*. If her purpose was to elicit complaints of racial discrimination and of the military generally, she was surely disappointed. A typical exchange went (in part) as follows:

Reporter: "Sergeant _____ said he was an anti-war protester in the early '70s, but in this conflict, he was prepared to die fighting for his country."

Sergeant: "It's my watch now. I had friends in the Nam, my father and relatives . . . were part of the Korean experience, I'm sure there were those in World War II or whatever it may be. And now it's my watch, and I want to be as honorable as they were and I want to participate in the campaign. I want to

share the American experience. I think when I go back, I can
start demanding whatever rights that I rate as a citizen. . . ."

This sergeant knew "what it means to be an American,"
and knew it well before President Clinton called for a conversation on the subject. Among other things, as Frederick
Douglass could have told him, it means to be a patriot. For
this we all, black and white, can thank Abraham Lincoln,
for it was he who saved, and in the process, restored the
Union in which the likes of Douglass could proudly be a patriot.

APPENDIX

Address Delivered at the Dedication of the Cemetery at
Gettysburg, November 19, 1863

Four score and seven years ago our fathers brought forth on
this continent, a new nation, conceived in Liberty, and dedicated to the proposition that all men are created equal.

Now we are engaged in a great civil war, testing whether
that nation, or any nation so conceived and so dedicated, can
long endure. We are met on a great battle-field of that war.
We have come to dedicate a portion of that field, as a final
resting place for those who here gave their lives that that nation might live. It is altogether fitting and proper that we
should do this.

But, in a larger sense, we can not dedicate—we can not
consecrate—we can not hallow—this ground. The brave
men, living and dead, who struggled here, have consecrated
it, far beyond our poor power to add or detract. The world
will little note, nor long remember what we say here, but it

can never forget what they did here. It is for us the living, rather, to be dedicated here to the unfinished work which they who fought here have thus far so nobly advanced. It is rather for us to be here dedicated to the great task remaining before us—that from these honored dead we take increased devotion to that cause for which they gave the last full measure of devotion—that we here highly resolve that these dead shall not have died in vain—that this nation, under God, shall have a new birth of freedom—and that government of the people, by the people, for the people, shall not perish from the earth.

THE PATRIOT'S FLAG

While we rally 'round the flag, boys,
Rally once again,
Shouting the Battle Cry of Freedom!

George F. Root

Although it has been amended, formally as well as by judicial interpretation, the Constitution written in 1787
has ordered the affairs of this nation for more than two hundred years. We have become so accustomed to it that we
might take its longevity for granted, but it is, in fact, remarkable, especially when compared with the experience of
other peoples. There are more now, but when I last had reason to look into this matter—in 1983, as a member of the
American delegation to the UN Commission on Human
Rights in Geneva—there were 164 countries in the world,
and all but six of them (Britain, New Zealand, Israel, Saudi
Arabia, Oman, and Libya) had written constitutions. But of
those 158 written constitutions, more than half had been

written after 1974, and, if the past is any guide, many of them will be rewritten or replaced in the future. France, for a conspicuous example, has had five republican constitutions in the period when we have had one, and, to update the old joke involving the cynical Paris taxi driver, "there'll be a sixth."

Many factors account for our success, not the least of them being the Constitution itself and the remarkably learned and talented men who drafted it. (Jefferson, in Paris at the time, called the Constitutional Convention an "assembly of demi-gods.") Then, unlike France, America did not have to deal with a sullen nobility, dispossessed by the revolution of its property and privileges but not of its hopes to regain them. (Tocqueville had this in mind when he said that the "great advantage of the Americans is that they arrived at a state of democracy without having to endure a democratic revolution, and that they [were] born equal instead of becoming so.") Unlike Poland, this country was not surrounded by powerful neighbors with hostile intentions; and (according to *Federalist* 2) it began with a people "speaking the same language" (unlike Belgium), "professing the same religion" (unlike what was Yugoslavia), "attached to the same principles of government" (unlike Spain), "very similar in their manners and customs" (unlike Canada), and a people who had established their general liberty and independence "by fighting side by side throughout a long and bloody war." Abraham Lincoln referred to them as "the patriots of seventy-six" and wondered whether the men of his time (and ours) would be prepared to do as they did. He had reason to wonder about this, especially because what they did in 1776 was to fight for a principle, or an idea, that later generations might take for granted or misunderstand.

I said in the first chapter of this book that patriotism

means love of country and implies a readiness to sacrifice for it, to fight for it, perhaps even to give one's life for it. But, aside from the legendary Spartans, why should anyone be willing to do this? Why, especially, should Americans be willing to do this? In theory, this nation began with self-interested men, by nature private men, men naturally endowed not with duties or obligations but with certain unalienable rights, the *private* rights to life, liberty, and the pursuit of a happiness that each defines for himself, and, again in theory, government is instituted only "to secure these rights." So, to repeat the question, why should self-interested men believe it in their interest to give their lives for the *idea* or *promise* of their country?

As one might expect, Lincoln provided the best answer to this question. I refer here, at least initially, not to the Gettysburg Address, or any other of his formal and famous speeches, but to an informal (in fact, extemporaneous) "address" delivered from the White House balcony to the men of the 166th Ohio regiment on the evening of August 22, 1864. He began by thanking them for their service to the country and continued by saying this:

I almost always feel inclined, when I happen to say anything to soldiers, to impress upon them in a few brief remarks the importance of success in this contest. It is not merely for to-day, but for all time to come that we should perpetuate for our children's children this great and free government, which we have enjoyed all our lives. I beg you to remember this, not merely for my sake, but for yours. I happen temporarily to occupy this big White House. I am a living witness that any one of your children may look to come here as my father's child has. It is in order that each of you may have through this free government which we have enjoyed, an open field and a fair chance for your industry, enterprise and intelligence: that you may all have equal privileges in the race of life, with all its desirable human aspirations. It is for this the struggle should be maintained, that we may not lose our birthright. . . . The nation is worth fighting for, to secure such an inestimable jewel.

Everything Lincoln says is true: their interests were bound up with the country's interests; in a way, their interests, if not identical with the country's interests, were dependent on them. But one has to wonder whether this argument would carry any weight with "the summer soldier and the sunshine patriot," who, as Thomas Paine wrote even in 1776, "will shrink from the service of their country." Such persons might see that the country deserves to be defended, but also that it is in their interest that someone else do the defending; their motto is, "Let George do it." Jean-Jacques Rousseau had these calculating men in mind when he said, in effect, that reasoning on the basis of self-interest alone would not lead anyone to put his life at risk for another or for his country.

The Founders were aware of this problem. They knew, and accepted as a fact, that the nation was formed by self-interested men, men, as John Locke puts it, naturally in a "state of perfect freedom to order their actions and dispose of their possessions and persons as they think fit . . . without asking leave or depending on the will of any other man." But they also knew, as Locke knew, that these men ceased to be autonomous, or simply self-interested men, when they entered civil society and agreed to be governed. That agreement made them citizens, and a citizen is obliged to think of his fellows and of the whole of which he is a part. This requires that he possess certain qualities of character, or virtues, and, as Madison says in *Federalist* 55, "republican government presupposes the existence of these qualities in a higher degree than any other form [of government]." Because these qualities cannot be taken for granted, they must somehow be cultivated.

So it was that Lincoln, as I explained at some length in chapter 5, used his words and the occasion of the Civil War to promote a love of country, reminding us that as citizens we are bound to each other and across the generations by a cause we hold in common, that there is a price to be paid for what he called (in his address to the Ohio regiment) "our birthright," and that we are indebted to those who have already paid it. So, too, a grateful nation erects monuments and memorials to him and the Founders, to the end that generations of Americans might stand in awe of them and of their words carved in the walls of the memorials; and it names its states, counties, cities, parks, boulevards, and schools after them. Their stories are the nation's story, and telling it should be the nation's business; in fact, it should be an important part of the civics curriculum in our schools. It is a way of inculcating in children a reverence for the past and its heroes, with the view of causing them to love their country. More generally, it is a way of preparing them to be citizens. We used to do all this, but it is rarely done today. Our schools teach "social studies," but neglect American history and biographies; and while our universities continue to offer courses in political theory, the theory taught is no longer what it was when Jefferson proposed the teaching of Locke's treatises and Sidney's discourses on government. Locke and Sidney, Montesquieu and even Rousseau, have given way to Marx, Nietzsche, and Heidegger, none of them a champion of constitutional government.

It is important to understand that America is the result of the coming together of theory and practice, and nowhere is this more evident than in the men who founded it. They were both political theorists and political practitioners, or, to put it differently, there was not then, as there is now, a division between intellectuals and politicians. The Declaration of Independence was drafted by Thomas Jefferson, John Adams, and Benjamin Franklin, men who had distinguished political careers, but who also wrote books and scientific papers, and founded universities (Jefferson, the University of Virginia; and Franklin, the Philadelphia Academy, which became the University of Pennsylvania). Not only that, but Franklin was one of the founders of our first so-called learned society (the American Philosophical Society), and Jefferson served as one of its first presidents. As for James Madison, Alexander Hamilton, and John Jay, they combined to write *The Federalist* (or *Federalist Papers*), which has been described in our own time as "the most important work in political science that has ever been written, or is likely ever to be written, in the United States."

But where there was once a unity there is now a division. Our politicians typically know nothing about what is going on in the world of political theory, and our theorists typically do not believe it part of their job to promote the cause of republican government. Some do—those who are not Marxists or "postmodernists"—but even they are likely to teach a version of republicanism different from that espoused by the Founders. There are no citizens in this new version, not in any meaningful sense, and no common good, only "autonomous" individuals, each with his own idiosyncratic view of the good. It follows—or is said to follow—that government may not put the weight of its authority behind any particular view of the good. On all such matters, it must be neutral or, as the current cant would have it, nonjudgmental.

This new republican theory made its first public appearance in the dissenting opinion written by Justice Oliver Wendell Holmes in a free speech case decided by the Supreme Court of the United States in 1925. Holmes said, and among libertarians became famous for saying, "If, in the long run, the beliefs expressed in proletarian dictatorship are destined to be accepted by the dominant forces of the community, the only meaning of free speech is that they should be given their chance and have their way." This view was repeated, again in a dissenting opinion, by Justice Hugo Black in a Communist Party case in 1961. As he put it, "education and contrary argument" may provide an adequate defense against communist (or fascist) speech, but if that "remedy is not sufficient," he added, echoing Holmes, "the only meaning of free speech must be that the revolutionary ideas will be allowed to prevail." First expressed by dissenters, this is now the accepted or prevailing view. The *only* meaning of free speech turns out to mean that it is worse to punish the advocacy of Stalinism or Hitlerism than to be ruled by a local Stalin or Hitler. This, quite obviously, could not have been the view held by James Madison and the other members of the Congress who drafted the First Amendment in 1789. They were sensible republicans.

Among other things, they knew what the Founders generally knew, and what they emphatically say in *Federalist* 2, namely, when instituting a government, the people are expected to surrender "some of their natural rights, in order to vest [the government] with requisite powers." But Holmes and Black are unmindful of this. Unlike Madison and the other authors of the First Amendment, they treat the constitutional right of freedom of speech as if it were a natural right, the right men possessed in the state of nature; there, as autonomous individuals, men might speak (and do) as they please without regard to political consequences because, there being no political community, nothing said (or done) could have political consequences. But, as the Founders made clear, that ceased to be the case when men entered civil society and formed a political community.

Under what is now the prevailing view of the First Amendment, however, men retain the right to speak as they please, regardless of the consequences of their speech, because the government is forbidden to weigh those consequences or take them into account. Just as Congress may not make any law favoring religion, especially one religion over another, so it may not favor, or put the weight of its authority behind, one or another view of republican government. Accordingly, while Americans, out of habit, might continue to "pledge allegiance to the flag of the United States of America, and to the Republic for which it stands," the Republic itself stands for nothing in particular, which means that the flag stands for nothing in particular. This, of course, was not the view of those who designed it. For them the flag, and its ceremonies, was one of the means of promoting patriotism.

The flag carried by the Continental army in January 1776 had thirteen stripes and the British ensign in the upper left-hand corner; but, after we declared our independence in July of that year, the Continental Congress resolved that "the flag of the thirteen United States be thirteen stripes, alternate red and white: that the union be thirteen stars, white in a blue field, representing a new constellation," which is to say, a new and different kind of country. Congress later declared the "Star-Spangled Banner" to be the national anthem, and June 14 to be Flag Day, and, later still, John Philip Sousa's " Stars and Stripes Forever" was designated the national march. As Madison indicated, republican government especially requires public-spiritedness, and Congress obviously intended the celebration of the flag—on Flag Day, for example—to be one of the means of promoting it.

In due course, the governments of the United States and forty-eight of the fifty states enacted statutes forbidding the burning (and, generally, the desecration) of the flag. They saw it as the symbol of this new country, this *novus ordo seclorum*, a country dedicated to the principles set down in the Declaration of Independence: liberty, equality of opportunity, and religious toleration. Its friends pledge allegiance to it and salute it, and its enemies burn it. (What better way to express contempt for the country than by burning its flag, or otherwise showing disrespect for it, for example, by spitting on it or by wearing it attached to the seat of one's trousers?) And when a person was tried and convicted under one of those statutes, the Supreme Court upheld the conviction, saying, "The state [of Nebraska] may exert its power to strengthen the bonds of Union, and therefore, to that end, may encourage patriotism and love of country among its people."

But this was said in 1907, before the new political theory took hold. In 1984, with his friends chanting, "America, the red, white, and blue, we spit on you," one Gregory Lee Johnson burned the American flag and was convicted under a Texas statute forbidding the desecration of a venerated object; and in 1989 the U.S. Supreme Court, by the narrowest of margins, declared the statute a violation of the First Amendment. Writing for the five-justice majority, Justice William Brennan said that Johnson's act was a form of expression, that the First Amendment protects the freedom of expression, that the Texas statute was not neutral insofar as it was aimed at this particular kind of expression, and, therefore, was unconstitutional.

This was sufficient to dispose of the case, but Brennan

went on for another five pages to argue that Johnson was convicted for exercising the "freedom that this cherished emblem represents." Like the American Civil Liberties Union, Brennan believes that the flag stands, above all, for freedom of expression, which implies that, by prohibiting Johnson from expressing himself, the state of Texas, not Johnson, had committed an offense against the flag. His argument, although not stated as such, takes the form of a syllogism: the flag stands for the Republic, the Republic stands for freedom of expression, therefore the flag stands for freedom of expression.

But the First Amendment protects freedom of speech, not expression, and, whereas all speech may be expression of a sort, not all expression is speech, and there is good reason why the framers of the First Amendment protected the one and not the other. A person can express himself in isolation, or (and it amounts to the same thing) by burning the flag or a draft card, by denouncing Catholics, or by marching through a Jewish neighborhood brandishing swastikas. But speech implies a listener—one speaks *to* someone—and, as well, the willingness to be a listener in return. In a word, speech implies conversation and, in the political realm especially, deliberation. It is a means of arriving at a decision, of bringing people together, which requires civility and mutual respect; and in a polity consisting of blacks and whites, Jews, Muslims, and Christians, liberals and conservatives, and peoples from every part of the globe, civility and mutual respect are a necessity. So understood, speech is good, which is why the Constitution protects it.

Even so, the flag and country obviously stand for more than freedom of speech (to say nothing of freedom of expression). Even Johnson knew this. He was part of a group gathered "to protest the policies of the Reagan administration and of certain Dallas-based corporations," which, of course, he was entitled to do; indeed, he would not have been arrested—not under the statute involved—had he burned an effigy of Ronald Reagan. (Reagan may be venerated in some quarters, but he is not a "venerated object.") Instead, he burned the flag, evidently because he wanted to show his contempt for it and, therefore, what it stands for. If, however, the right to speak freely, or even to express oneself, is all it stands for, he could not have shown his contempt for it by exercising the freedom for which it stands. In that circumstance, he would be paying tribute to it; and that, surely, is not what he intended to do.

I do not mean to belittle the importance of freedom of speech; as I suggested above, it is an essential feature of republican government. I mean only to say that the flag stands for *every*thing the country stands for, and, therefore, that Brennan's understanding of it is partial or incomplete. As such, it cannot explain why it is, as Brennan said it was, a "cherished emblem." It cannot explain why, for example, the Marines on Iwo Jima, where some six thousand of them died fighting for their country, raised the flag on Mount Suribachi, in fact (as we know from the famous photograph, and especially from the Marine Corps Memorial in the Arlington National Cemetery), struggled to raise it on the only staff available to them, a piece of battlefield pipe. Nor can it explain why it was thought appropriate to drape the flag over the body of the Marine sergeant killed in the 1998 bombing of our embassy in Nairobi, Kenya, or why the embassy staff—I'm quoting the Marine Corps report—"stood erect and silent as the body was removed from the rubble and placed in a waiting vehicle." The fact is, the flag is used to express what is in the hearts and minds of most Americans on such occasions. The chief justice said as much when, in his dissenting opinion in the *Johnson* case, he spoke of "the deep awe and respect for our flag felt by virtually all of us." We are, as the chief justice suggests, emotionally attached to it.

For it is our emotions, more than our rational faculties, that are triggered by the sight of the flag, not when it is used (or abused) for commercial purposes, but when it is waved and flown on Flag Day and the Fourth of July, and displayed at the various war memorials on the Mall in Washington or, for that matter, in towns and cities around the country, and on the battlefields at Bull Run, Antietam, and Gettysburg, and at the cemeteries where those who fought and died are buried, not only at Arlington and Gettysburg, but in the faraway places we sometimes visit, among them, Manila in the Philippines, Cambridge in England, Château-Thierry in the north of France, and, perhaps most famously, above Omaha Beach in Normandy. The sight of it, especially in these places, evokes memories of past battles and of those who fought them, and to whom we are indebted. They served our country and were the better for it; by honoring them, as we do, we pay a service of our own and are the better for it. I can make this point with an analogy: not every American can be a Lincoln, but all Americans are made better by reading his words and coming to love him and the cause for which he gave his life.

To the end that we remember him, and by remembering, come to love him, the government authorized the building of the Lincoln Memorial; and no one, I think, not even the most zealous civil libertarian, would argue that the Johnsons among us are free to express themselves by spraying it with graffiti. There is something about the memorial that forbids its desecration, and, because it, too, causes us to remember, the same ought to be true of the flag.

As it happens, no one is burning the flag these days, not because everyone has come to respect it, but because, since flag-desecration is no longer illegal, there is now no point in burning it. Whatever its intentions, the Supreme Court has succeeded in putting the Johnsons among us out of business, or, at least, out of the flag-burning business. Nevertheless, efforts have been made to amend the Constitution, giving Congress the authority to "prohibit the physical desecration of the flag of the United States," and, according to the public opinion polls, something like two-thirds of the American people favor its adoption. But I doubt that any good can come of it. It can be adopted only over the disdainful opposition of intellectuals in the national press, the law schools, and, of course, the American Civil Liberties Union, and, whatever its outcome, the debate will be nasty and serve no good purpose. Better, then, to leave well enough alone.

The four dissenters in the second of the flag-burning cases (*United States* v. *Eichman*) said they feared, partly as a result of the Court's decision in the *Johnson* case, that "the symbolic value of the American flag is not the same today as it was yesterday," and that Americans living today would have "difficulty understanding the message [it] conveyed to their parents and grandparents." But there is reason to believe their fears are exaggerated. As is made clear in the epilogue that follows this chapter, the flag continues to be treated by some Americans with the respect it deserves, and most Americans, I should like to think, will be moved by the story recounted in it, just as they were moved by the film *Saving Private Ryan* with its scenes of the flags in the cemetery in Normandy.

———

The country has had its share of summer soldiers and sunshine patriots, but they were few compared with the millions of Americans who, over the course of our history, have willingly put their lives at risk for the country and its principles. We know little about them save for that fact, and that they must have wanted the country to endure. (Why, else, would they have fought for it?) But to know that they wanted the country to endure is to know something else about them; in fact, it is to know something of importance about them: that they felt themselves obligated to their forefathers and their posterity, the forebearers because, from them, they had inherited a country worth fighting and dying for, this "inestimable jewel," as Lincoln referred to it, and their posterity because, being related to them, by nationality if not by blood, they were anxious that they, too, might enjoy its many benefits.

It seems almost naive to speak of these things at a time when Americans are told in their schools that all "cultures" are equal, that there is nothing special about their country and, therefore, no good reason to admire the men who founded it; and told by the highest court in the land that the flag stands for freedom of speech and opinion, meaning any speech and any opinion, because none is better or more valid than any other.

But this nation was not founded on an opinion. The men who declared our independence said, "We hold these truths to be self-evident," and in support of this declaration they pledged their lives, their fortunes, and their sacred honor. No one would make this pledge in support of an opinion, knowing it to be merely an opinion and, therefore, no more worthy of respect than its opposite. Would Americans have fought for the Union—and 359,528 of them died fighting for it—if they had been taught in their schools that the Union was founded on nothing more than an *opinion* concerning human nature and the rights affixed to it? Not likely; but fight they did, and for that we honor them.

Because of them, and the patriots who followed them at Normandy and Bastogne, Guadalcanal and Iwo Jima, Midway and the Coral Sea, Korea and Kuwait, and, yes, even Vietnam, this country has endured, and with it has endured "the last, best hope of earth." This, I firmly believe, is as true now as it was when Lincoln first said it in 1862.

EPILOGUE

—·—

The following story is told by a foreign diplomat who, as he explains, had occasion to visit the United States Embassy in the capital of his country.

—·—

"I arrived at a quarter to six, after official office hours, and was met by the Marine on guard at the entrance of the Chancery. He asked if I would mind waiting while he lowered the two American flags at the Embassy. What I witnessed over the next ten minutes so impressed me that I am now led to make this occurrence a part of my ongoing record of this distressing era.

"The Marine was dressed in a uniform which was spotless and neat; he walked with a measured tread from the entrance of the Chancery to the stainless steel flagpole before the Embassy and, almost reverently, lowered the flag to the level of his reach where he began to fold it in military fashion. He then released the flag from the clasps attaching it to the rope, stepped back from the pole, made an about-face, and carried the flag between his hands—one above, one below—and placed it securely on a stand before the Chancery.

"He then marched over to the second flagpole and repeated the same lonesome ceremony. . . . After completing his task, he apologized for the delay—out of pure courtesy, as nothing less than incapacity would have prevented him from fulfilling his goal—and said to me, 'Thank you for waiting, Sir. I had to pay honor to my country.'

"I have had to tell this story because there was something impressive about a lone Marine carrying out a ceremonial task which obviously meant very much to him and which, in its simplicity, made the might, the power and the glory of the United States of America stand forth in a way that a mighty wave of military aircraft, or the passage of a super-carrier, or a parade of 10,000 men could never have made manifest.

"One day it is my hope to visit one of our embassies in a faraway place and to see a soldier fold our flag and turn to a stranger and say, 'I am sorry for the delay, Sir. I had to honor my country.'"*

*From "Commentary: Diplomat Notices Marine's Patriotism," *The Scout* (Camp Pendleton Military Base), May 28, 1998. Reprinted by permission.

INDEX OF NAMES

———•———